DISCOVER CANADA

# New Brunswick

By Marjorie Gann

**Consultants**

**Desmond Morton, FRSC,** Professor of History, University of Toronto

**Geoff Martin, Ph.D.,** Centre for Canadian Studies,
Mount Allison University, Sackville

**John G. Reid,** Professor of History,
Saint Mary's University, Halifax

**Léon Thériault,** Département d'histoire et de géographie,
Université de Moncton

Grolier Limited
TORONTO

**Many small New Brunswick towns and villages are built around their churches.
This one is St. André in the Saint John River Valley.**
*Overleaf:* **The Bay of Fundy, seen from Cape Enrage**

**Canadian Cataloguing in Publication Data**

Gann, Marjorie
  New Brunswick

(Discover Canada)
Includes index.
ISBN 0-7172-2721-9

1. New Brunswick — Juvenile literature. I. Title.
II. Series: Discover Canada (Toronto, Ont.).

FC2461.2.G3 1994    971.5′1    C94-930921-4
F1042.4.G73 1994

**Front cover:** Restored sawmill at Kings Landing
Historical Settlement near Fredericton
**Back cover:** *Lower Forty Five No. 1,* covered bridge
in Fundy National Park

Printed and bound in Canada.
Published simultaneously in the United States.
1 2 3 4 5 6 7 8 9 10  DWF  99 98 97 96 95 94

A tranquil farm scene near Holderville on the Long Reach, Saint John River. This 32 kilometre (20-mile) stretch of the river is flanked by hills covered with hardwood forests and laced with trout streams.

## Table of Contents

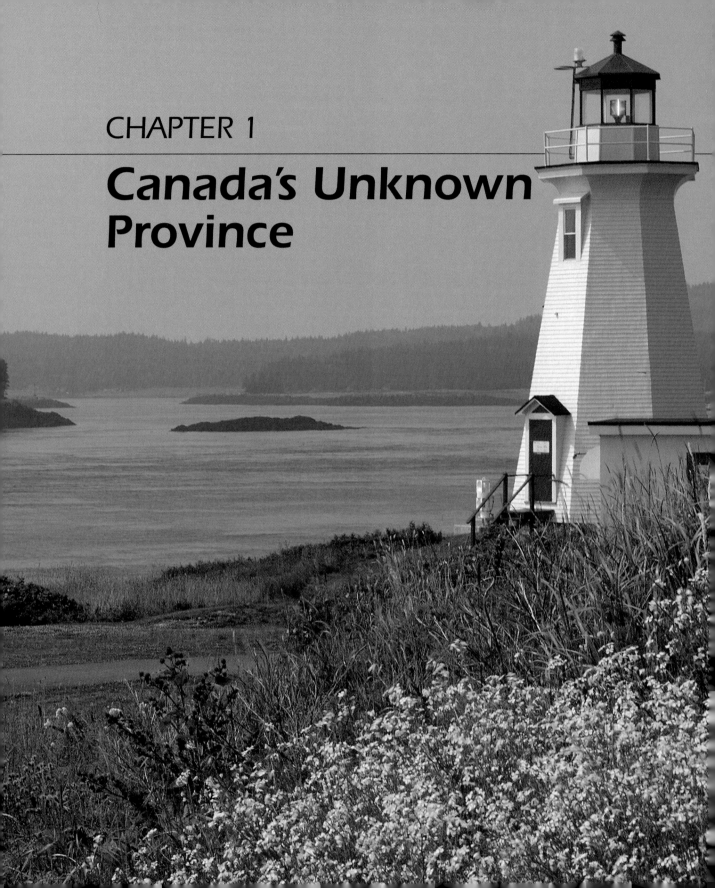

# CHAPTER 1
# Canada's Unknown Province

New Brunswick is the Canadian province that's easy to miss. Tourists on their way to the east coast have a tendency to drive through it without stopping to take a good look around. Yet, like a shy person who is worth getting to know, New Brunswick hides treasures that are worth seeking out.

From the unspoiled beaches of its Atlantic shoreline through the wilderness of its interior highlands to the rugged Fundy coast, the province offers a range of scenery to explore. Salt marshes and forests attract hundreds of species of birds, and whales and other sea mammals can be seen near the islands that stud the southern coast.

If New Brunswick's beauty is easy to overlook, so is its history, which was determined by forces as powerful as the high tides that sweep through the Bay of Fundy twice a day. Five hundred years ago, the Micmac and Maliseet people hunted and fished throughout the province. Later, France and Britain fought over it. The Acadian settlers were driven out in 1755, only to return to become today's vibrant Acadian community. Now New Brunswickers of Native, French and British heritage, together with immigrants from many parts of the world, contribute to the province's cultural richness.

For a small province, New Brunswick has produced a remarkable number of accomplished figures of national stature — renowned painters and writers, important scientists and inventors, innovative businesspeople, and colourful politicians. Some have had to leave to succeed, but many have found stimulation and opportunity at home, in a province of exceptional beauty, an abundance of natural resources, and a rich and fascinating history.

**Green Point lighthouse at Letete, the ferry landing for Deer Island**

# CHAPTER 2
# The Land

**W**edged between land and water, New Brunswick links continental North America with Canada's other two Maritime provinces, Nova Scotia and Prince Edward Island. The Isthmus of Chignecto is the province's land bridge to mainland Nova Scotia. Another bridge, the long-awaited Fixed Link, will soon span the Northumberland Strait from Cape Tormentine on New Brunswick's easternmost tip to Borden, Prince Edward Island. New Brunswick shares long land borders with Quebec on the north and the state of Maine on the west. Its other half is bounded by water — the Bay of Chaleur on the north, the Bay of Fundy on the south, and the Gulf of St. Lawrence and Northumberland Strait in between. Indeed, land and sea have shaped New Brunswick in many ways, from its earliest days to the present.

## The Shape of the Land

New Brunswick is not a large province. With an area of 73 437 square kilometres (28 354 square miles), it is the third smallest in Canada. But its terrain is remarkably varied.

If you flew low over New Brunswick in an airplane, you would immediately be struck by the amount of tree cover and the number of lakes and rivers deposited by the glaciers of the last Ice Age. Forests blanket almost 90 percent of the land with softwood trees like white pine, spruce and balsam fir, and hardwoods like maple, ash and yellow birch.

A brilliant display of autumn colours in the New Brunswick interior, one of the most densely forested regions in the world

For a small province, New Brunswick presents a remarkable variety of landscapes. Seen here: *(above)* Mount Carleton, in the Central Highlands, the highest point in the province; *(top right)* low-lying islands in the Saint John River at Lower Jemseg; *(right)* Pokeshaw Provincial Park on the Bay of Chaleur

Despite the amount of forest, New Brunswick is divided into a few distinct regions whose landscapes vary enormously.

The Central Highlands region, which slopes eastward to form the Coastal Lowlands, is a northern extension of the Appalachian Mountain Range, formed about 380 million years ago. Its highest peak, Mount Carleton, is 820 metres (2690 feet) high. There are two other hilly regions — the Southern Highlands, whose hills slope gently down to the Bay of Fundy, and the Northern Uplands.

Nothing has shaped the province's contrasting landscapes like its waters — its many rivers, and the Atlantic Ocean. The Saint John River, the province's longest, flows 673 kilometres (418 miles) from the uplands of Maine through a hilly, fertile green valley, past

The famous "Flowerpot Rocks" at Hopewell Cape on the Fundy Coast — *(below)* at low tide, and *(left)* when the tide is in

countless potato fields, into the Bay of Fundy. Wilder by far is the forested landscape crisscrossed by the province's other rivers, including the Restigouche in the Northern Uplands and the Miramichi, with its numerous tributaries, in the interior.

Fundy's powerful tides have sculpted the red conglomerate cliffs at Hopewell Cape into strange, rocky apparitions resembling giant, tree-crowned flowerpots which turn into small, rocky islands when the tide comes in. Elsewhere along the Fundy Coast are the reddish mud flats and grassy salt marshes of Chignecto Bay. Off the southwestern tip of the province are Deer and Campobello islands and imposing Grand Manan, whose stark basalt cliffs were born of volcanic lava millions of years ago.

The warmer waters of the Gulf of St. Lawrence and the Bay of Chaleur form sheltered lagoons. At the northeastern tip of this region stands tranquil Miscou Island, whose white dunes invite the rare piping plover to nest, and whose sparsely treed peat bogs support breeding palm warblers.

## Climate

Although New Brunswick is a Maritime province, its climate is as much influenced by the dry air from the continent as by the moderating influences of the sea. Combined with the sea air that surrounds New Brunswick, this continental *prevailing wind* makes for sharp temperature variations. Coastal areas are warmer in winter and cooler in summer than inland areas. If you leave Fredericton for PEI on a hot July day, you may have to put on a windbreaker at the Cape Tormentine ferry terminal, where the temperature may be several degrees cooler.

Winter sees more precipitation than any other season, and New Brunswick's southern coast gets the most. When a monster snowstorm hit southern New Brunswick in 1992, it snowed for four days, dumping 160 centimetres (more than 5 feet) on Moncton, the heaviest total for a single storm since record keeping began in 1881.

*Below:* **Early morning fog at Chance Harbour in the Saint John area.** *Right:* **A sparkling winter day in Fundy National Park.** *Bottom right:* **Accident on the Trans-Canada Highway during the record-breaking storm of 1992**

Far from complaining, New Brunswickers soldiered on with tremendous good humour. With the help of volunteers with four-wheel-drive vehicles, the Victorian Order of Nurses continued to visit the sick, and Meals on Wheels made regular deliveries.

New Brunswickers are used to hearing weather announcers call for "fog along the Fundy coast," especially in summer. As renowned in Canada as London's fog is in Europe, Fundy fog forms when moist air warmed by the land moves over the cooler bay. On a given day, the coastal and inland weather may differ markedly — warm and sunny inland, cool and foggy on the coast. This means that coastal forests are less susceptible to forest fires, and coastal red spruces grow exceptionally tall.

## Tides and Salt Marshes

Fundy's tides are the highest in the world. Where inlets in the bay are narrowest — as they are at Moncton, in the long, narrow estuary of the Petitcodiac River — the tide forms a wave called a *tidal bore*.

The bay's water rocks naturally from head to mouth and back again about every 13 hours in a motion called a *seiche*. Together, this seiche, the ocean tides and the bay's funnel shape generate Fundy's exceptional tides, higher than 15 metres (49 feet) at the head. For comparison, the tidal ranges in other high-tide locations, like St. Malo in France or Bristol in England, are only 10 metres (33 feet). Fundy's daily discharge is estimated to equal that of all the rivers in the world.

The tides have produced a broad expanse of salt marshes — 357 square kilometres (138 square miles) before human encroachment. Far from being wastelands, these coastal wetlands are crucial to the food cycle, breaking down nutritionally rich plant and animal matter that the tides return to the ocean. Herring, flounder, scallops and mussels are nurtured here, great blue herons fish here, the American coot roosts here, and the black duck winters over.

Mud flats along the Petitcodiac River. They are left behind by the famous tidal bore — a high wave that surges up the river and then recedes with the twice-daily rise and fall of the Fundy tides.

Even mammals rely on salt marshes; raccoons munch on the clams and shrimp, and deer feed on the salty stems in the winter.

## Wildlife

New Brunswick's fields, forests, valleys and coastlines invite a wide array of birdlife; almost 40 percent of all species recorded in North America have been sighted here. In late summer, birdwatchers flock to the shores of Shepody Bay, a Fundy inlet, to view the hundreds of thousands of semipalmated sandpipers that come to feed on the fat mud shrimp at low tide, before taking off again for a 4600-kilometre (2860-mile) non-stop flight to South America. Known locally as "the peeps," these tiny shore birds are best seen at high tide, when they cluster together like a pebbled grey carpet on the narrow shore. On rocky, treeless Machias Seal Island, a bird sanctuary that can be reached by boat from Grand Manan, 900 pairs of nesting Atlantic puffins gather. Snowy owls can be sighted in the Tantramar Marshes near Sackville, and bald eagles at the Mactaquac Dam on the Saint John River near Fredericton. New Brunswick is also home to such endangered species as the peregrine falcon, recently reintroduced at Fundy Park.

Passing motorists often catch a glimpse of browsing moose, which the Natives valued for food, clothing and shelter, as close to

An abundance of wildflowers and vast numbers of visiting and resident birds (seen here, a snowy owl and an American coot with its chick) are just two of the attractions of Deer Island, off the southwestern tip of the province. Another is the opportunity to see the several species of whales that visit the Bay of Fundy.

civilization as the woods just outside the capital, Fredericton. More numerous are the white-tailed deer, few in number until the turn of the century. Coyotes, unknown in the province until recently, are now a nuisance to sheep farmers. Other mammals include the black bear, bobcat, lynx and red fox and the porcupine, which the Micmacs hunted as much for their decorative quills as for their meat.

In New Brunswick, you don't have to go to an aquarium to see whales. Boatloads of tourists leave Grand Manan and other islands to view cavorting dolphins, as many as 500 in a pod, and the 24-metre (78-foot) finback, the second largest whale in the world. The clown of the sea, the humpback, with bumps on its flippers and knobs on its snout, makes an occasional appearance as well.

Tourists also come to fish for the famed Atlantic salmon, the acrobatic smallmouth bass, shad, brook trout and pickerel along the province's sprawling river system, which includes the Miramichi, the Nepisiguit, the Tobique and the Saint John. Sadly, years of overfishing, poor logging practices, acid rain and dam construction have depleted the stocks.

## Pollution and the Environment

The New Brunswick economy relies heavily on the health of the province's natural resources. The forest industry creates one in every eight jobs; more than 20 000 New Brunswickers make a living from the fishery; and the hunting, fishing and hiking made possible by New Brunswick's woods, lakes, streams and beaches support an important tourist industry.

For too long New Brunswickers have neglected these resources. Clear-cutting and inadequate replanting have reduced the size of forests, home to more than 31 000 species of plants and animals. More than 230 of these are considered to be endangered, threatened or rare. Acid rain, chemical spraying, chemical fertilizers and

New Brunswickers are very concerned about the health of their forests and waters and of the animals — like this white-tailed deer — that depend on them. Not only have several protected areas been established, but park wardens and others are involved in ongoing studies to monitor the status of threatened species.

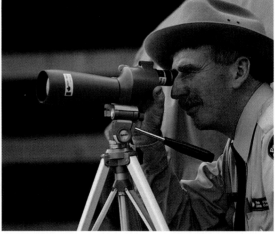

16

wastes from pulp and paper mills have damaged forests or polluted lakes and rivers. Although New Brunswick committed itself to nuclear power in 1970 with the construction of the Point Lepreau Nuclear Generating Station, this form of energy has remained controversial. Some people are concerned about the risk of accidents and the disposal of nuclear wastes, while others see it as a safe, clean alternative to oil and hydroelectric power.

The New Brunswick government appointed a "Premier's Round Table on Environment and Economy" in 1988. Calling for "sustainable development," this group pointed out that conservation of all resources is essential to the health of the province's economy and people. It recommended many measures, including education, the protection of lakes, rivers and shorelines from degradation, and the designation of various regions of the province as protected ecological areas.

The wide boardwalks of Kouchibouguac National Park protect the sand dunes, marsh grasses and nests of endangered piping plovers. Those who walk them can get close to nature without damaging the fragile environment. Lagoons, salt marshes and peat bogs nestled behind the dunes are the most productive eco-system in the world.

# CHAPTER 3

# Early History

**N**o one knows for certain when the first people came to live in the land we now call New Brunswick. Archaeologists agree, however, that people moved into the area soon after the last Ice Age ended about 10 600 years ago.

When the first European explorers and traders arrived in New Brunswick in the sixteenth and seventeenth centuries, they met two distinct but related peoples, the Micmacs and the Maliseets, who were also closely related to the Passamaquoddy, Penobscot and Abnaki peoples of what is now the state of Maine. The Maliseets lived on the Saint John River and called themselves Wool-us'-te-goo-geu-wi'-uk, meaning "people of beautiful river." The Micmacs, whose name is thought to mean "my kin-friends," lived on the rivers and coasts of what is now eastern New Brunswick, Nova Scotia, Prince Edward Island and the Gaspé region of Quebec.

The two groups spoke closely related Algonkian languages that are still spoken in many Maritime Native communities. The Algonkian language group, to which they belong, stretches from the Atlantic provinces and New England as far as the Rocky Mountains.

Some of the early Europeans were so impressed with the Native way of life they wrote detailed accounts of what they observed. Among them were lawyer Marc Lescarbot and Jesuit missionary Pierre Biard, who described both Micmacs and Maliseets. In 1672, French fur trader Nicolas Denys described moose hunts, wigwam- and canoe-building, and Micmac family life. John Gyles, an English

**Fort Frederick, detail of a painting by Thomas Davies. Built by the British in 1758, the fort was one of several attempts by Europeans to create a permanent settlement at the site of present-day Saint John.**

boy captured by Maliseets in 1689, wrote of corn cultivation, hunting, fishing, ceremonies and cures, such as the sweat lodge and the use of fir balsam to treat frostbite.

The Micmacs and Maliseets lived a migratory life, following their food supply between the coast and the forest. In winter, they formed small bands to hunt moose, bear, caribou and small game like beaver and otter. With spring came the move downriver to fish for salmon and gather shellfish. Children collected sea birds' eggs and berries, which the women dried into cakes for the winter.

They were great conservationists; a successful moose hunt provided meat, hides for clothing and moccasins, "moose butter" for soups, bones for tools and sinews for sewing. Birch bark was fashioned into canoes, wigwam coverings and containers.

We know that Maliseet women planted corn, beans and pumpkins. English settlers, however, drove them off their planting grounds near the end of the eighteenth century.

Under the Native system of government, all people participated in decisions through the process of consensus. Discussing issues until there was no serious disagreement tended to promote harmony and co-operation. When leaders were needed for important tasks they were chosen in this way.

For entertainment, there was dancing, singing and story-telling, including tales about Ableegomooch, the trickster rabbit, and the great hero Glooscap, who as the first human used his great powers for the good of the people. These oral traditions taught children the values needed for survival — sharing, co-operation and respect for all sources of life, including the earth, water, plants, animals and fish. In this way children learned to conserve resources for future generations.

## Explorers

Spanish, French and English people often think of themselves as the "discoverers" of America, although Native people had been here for thousands of years before European explorers arrived. The first Europeans the Natives met were probably Norse explorers from Iceland and Greenland who arrived about the year 1000. According to Norse sagas, men like Bjarni Herjolfsson and Leif Ericsson sailed their longboats westward, explored the Atlantic coast, and even established short-lived settlements there. Since Ericsson's crew cut a cargo of vines to use in shipbuilding, stories arose about a legendary "Vinland." Its precise location remains uncertain, although archaeological evidence of Norse settlements has been found in Newfoundland.

It was not until 500 years later that European exploration began in earnest. Around the year 1500, ambitious European rulers began to expand their empires. They sent explorers westward across the Atlantic Ocean in hopes of discovering gold or silver or a fast route to the Spice Islands of Asia.

In 1497 and 1498, the Italian Giovanni Caboto, also known as John Cabot, landed on the northeast coast of North America at Newfoundland or Cape Breton, claiming the area on behalf of Henry

VII of England. His reports of a sea teeming with fish energized English, French, Spanish, Portuguese and Basque fishermen, who began fishing Newfoundland's Grand Banks, especially for cod. The fish was often dried on shore, leading to contact and trade with the Native people, and sometimes to conflict.

France employed another Italian, Giovanni da Verrazzano, in 1524. He was the first explorer to recognize that the entire coast of North America, from Florida to the Gulf of St. Lawrence, belonged to a single body of land.

Ten years later, Jacques Cartier left the French port of St. Malo and explored the northern coast of the Gulf of St. Lawrence, returning again in 1535 and 1541. Cartier met and traded with various Native peoples as he explored the Bay of Chaleur ("Bay of Heat"), which he named for the warmth of its waters. On his first voyage up the St. Lawrence as far as the Iroquoian settlements of Stadacona (today's Quebec City) and Hochelaga (Montreal), he captured several Natives, taking them to Europe. This, and the explorers' practice of laying claim to the lands they charted, aroused distrust of Europeans among Native peoples.

## Early Settlement

Yet trade grew rapidly between Europeans and natives. The Europeans wanted furs, especially beaver pelts for the hats that were in fashion; the Natives valued the Europeans' iron tools, copper kettles and cloth.

To secure this trade, the Europeans decided to establish some permanent settlements. One of the first attempts was made in 1604 by 79 Frenchmen, under the leadership of Pierre du Gua, Sieur de Monts, accompanied by navigator and geographer Samuel de Champlain. Initially, they explored the Bay of Fundy, which they named "La Baye Française," and the mouth of the Saint John River. They settled on an island in Passamaquoddy Bay, which they called "Île Ste-Croix" (St. Croix Island in English today), hoping its

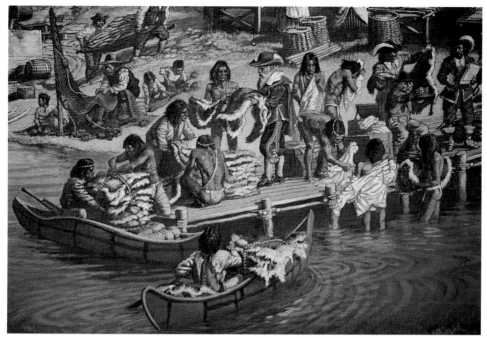

**Micmac and French traders examine each others' goods in the early 1700s.**

location would protect them against attacks by the English and the Native peoples.

They chose poorly. Their crops failed in the sandy topsoil. They had to cut down the surrounding cedars for firewood, losing their protection as a windbreak. There was no source of fresh water, their cider froze, and they failed to seek help from the Natives, whom they did not trust. By winter's end, half the men had died of scurvy. When a ship arrived from France with fresh supplies in spring, de Monts moved the settlement to Port Royal in Nova Scotia's fertile Annapolis Valley. Although this new settlement did not endure, the French based their claim to the region on its brief occupation between 1605 and 1613, when it was attacked by a raiding party from the English colony of Jamestown, Virginia.

Two decades later, French settlers, or "Acadians," as they came to be known, would establish villages along the marshes of the Bay of Fundy and throughout Acadia, today's Maritime Provinces. Two derivations have been suggested for the name "Acadia" ("Acadie" in French). Many historians think it came from the name "Arcadia," which designated an idealized period in antiquity, applied by the explorer Verrazzano to the American coast further south (Delaware, Maryland and Virginia); others relate it to the Micmac word "quoddy" or "cady," meaning a piece of land. Whatever the source, the name was in common use by the early 1700s.

To encourage settlement in Acadia, the French government granted tracts of land to noblemen. These gentlemen brought over settlers for whom they were to provide supplies and services — roads, mills and protection. In exchange for trading and fishing rights, the settlers were expected to work the land and pay rent to the *seigneur,* or lord.

In the New Brunswick part of Acadia, the French established about 34 *seigneuries,* although few were actually settled. Three of the most famous of the *seigneurs* were Charles de La Tour, Nicolas Denys and Charles de Menou d'Aulnay de Charnisay. Denys was awarded land on the Bay of Chaleur, on the Miramichi River and in Richibucto. He built up a fish, fur and timber trading post at Miscou and brought over Jesuit missionaries to convert the Natives to Christianity. Denys' account of his 40 years in Acadia, *Natural History of the People, Animal and Plant Life of North America and Its Climate,* paints a vivid picture of how the Micmacs lived at the time of early contact with Europeans.

For his part, d'Aulnay had sponsored some 50 families and hired hands from France. He and Charles de La Tour were rivals for control of the fur trade along the Saint John River. When d'Aulnay attacked La Tour's fort in his absence (1645), Madame de La Tour courageously led the defense. Forced to surrender, she soon died. In a curious twist, d'Aulnay died in a canoeing accident five years later, and La Tour regained control of the trade by marrying d'Aulnay's widow.

While the *seigneurs* were wrangling over control of Acadia, the French and English governments were doing the same. By the time the King of France gave Acadia to the British in the Treaty of Utrecht in 1713, the territory had shifted hands seven times.

Madame de La Tour pleading with d'Aulnay to spare the lives of her soldiers. Merciless, he forced her to watch as they were hanged. She died in prison three weeks later.

## Native People

Meanwhile, the Micmac and Maliseet people themselves never surrendered their lands. They welcomed traders but vigorously objected to encroachment on their territory, especially when access to their hunting and fishing grounds was cut off.

Acadian settlement, on the coasts or the marshes bordering the main rivers, did not interfere unduly with Native hunting and fishing patterns. An amicable French-Micmac relationship developed, further cemented by Micmac conversion to Catholicism.

English settlement, on the other hand, spread rapidly up the coast from Massachusetts into what is now Maine, threatening the Natives' livelihood. Yet when the Abnakis and Penobscots complained, they were generally ignored by the colonial authorities. In the six wars that ensued between Natives and colonists in the Maine-Maritime region from 1675 to 1765, the Micmacs and Maliseets usually assisted their cousins to the south, even when their own land interests were not directly affected.

## The Acadians

Often ignored by governments and seigneurs alike, the Acadian settlers came to rely more and more on themselves. They expanded to new lands on their own initiative, and chose their own leaders. Because many were related by blood or marriage, they thought of themselves as a distinct community. They had large families, often with ten to twelve children.

Although the main centres of Acadian settlement were along the Minas Basin of Nova Scotia and at Beaubassin on the Isthmus of

Trade between Acadia and New England flourished in the mid 1600s in spite of the fact that the colonies belonged to rival European countries that were often at war.

Chignecto, there were also outposts in what is now the New Brunswick mainland — Le Coude on the Petitcodiac River, Memramcou on the Memramcook River, Chipoudy on Shepody Bay and Jemseg and Sainte-Anne (Fredericton) on the Saint John River. And there were scantily populated forts, fishing ports and fur trading posts.

Despite the political turmoil surrounding them, life was good for the Acadians. Dyking the marshes in the Minas Basin of Nova Scotia and along the Chignecto Isthmus allowed them to farm the rich soil. It also helped to build a strong sense of community.

The fertile marshland yielded good crops of corn, wheat, rye, peas, oats, and flax that the women spun into linen. The Acadians also raised cattle, sheep and pigs, hunted small game, built weirs to catch gaspereaux and other fish, and planted apple orchards as they had done in France. An added bonus — a thriving illegal trade of farm products, furs and fish with the New England colonies — made the Acadians economically self-sufficient.

Although they were French, the Acadians' loyalty was not necessarily to the French government, but to their families, their villages and their land. In fact, although the French tried to persuade them to move to French-controlled territory after 1713, most Acadians stayed put. The British were happy to have them stay to supply the garrisons and develop the land, as long as they remained loyal to the Crown.

From 1713 until 1755, successive British governors attempted to convince the Acadian leaders to prove their loyalty by signing an oath of allegiance. For their part, the Acadians insisted that they were loyal to the Crown, but refused to sign an unconditional oath that would require them to bear arms against the French.

Curiously, in 1751 the *French* commander at Fortress Louisbourg on Île Royale (Cape Breton) insisted on an oath of loyalty from the Acadians who had moved there, labelling them "rebels" for refusing to fight on the *French* side. Caught between two world powers, the Acadians chose to remain neutral.

**Inside Fort Beauséjour in the spring of 1754**

The Acadians did sign an oath of loyalty in 1729-30, when Governor Richard Philipps promised to exempt them from bearing arms. By the 1740s, however, the conflict between France and Britain was heating up. The British began constructing Fort Lawrence, on the Chignecto Isthmus, in 1750; by 1751, the French had begun work on Fort Beauséjour, on the opposite side of the Missaguash River.

With Major Charles Lawrence's appointment as lieutenant-governor in 1753, official tolerance for Acadian neutrality came to an abrupt end. Backed by Governor Shirley of Massachusetts and other authorities, he announced that the Acadians must sign an unconditional oath or leave.

A large force of British and New Englanders attacked Beauséjour in early June of 1755. When the fort fell, about 200 armed Acadians were found among the defenders. Whether they were there freely or had been forced to fight, as they claimed, is unknown.

## The Expulsion of the Acadians

Once again, Lawrence presented the Acadians with an unconditional oath to sign. When they refused, he set in motion a tragic episode in Canadian history — the expulsion of the Acadian people from the land they cherished.

Since Lawrence wanted to leave the Acadians nothing to come back to, the men were rounded up to prevent them from rescuing their cattle, and their farms were burnt. Some Acadians, including women and children, escaped to the woods, where many were later found and deported; others fled to Quebec. But most were put on boats and shipped off to the British colonies — New York, Pennsylvania, Massachusetts, Maryland, Virginia, the Carolinas, Georgia. Many died en route. The ship *The Cornwallis* left Chignecto for South Carolina with 417 on board; it arrived with only 210 alive. The *Violet* and the *Duke William*, with hundreds on board, were lost at sea.

Some of the British officers charged with organizing the deportation found their duty painful. Addressing a group of assembled Acadian men and boys, Lieutenant-colonel John Winslow said: "The part of duty I am now upon is very disagreeable to my natural make and temper, as I know it must be grievous to you....I Shall do everything in my power...[to] make this remove, which I am sensible must give you a great deal of trouble, as easy as his Majesty's service will admit."

Although there is no evidence that the British authorities deliberately attempted to break up families, we do know that Governor Lawrence impatiently ordered the general in charge, "I would have you not wait for the wives and children coming in but ship off the men without them." In some cases the large Acadian families were separated in the chaos and confusion, with brothers and sisters, grandparents and grandchildren, ending up on boats bound for separate destinations.

The exiled Acadians did not adapt to their new surroundings or settle in small groups as the British had hoped. Instead, many wandered from colony to colony in search of lost family. Many died, and others went to the French colony of Louisiana. The settlers shipped to the Virginia colony were promptly dispatched to England, which they left for France. Many of these later recrossed the Atlantic to join other Acadians in Louisiana.

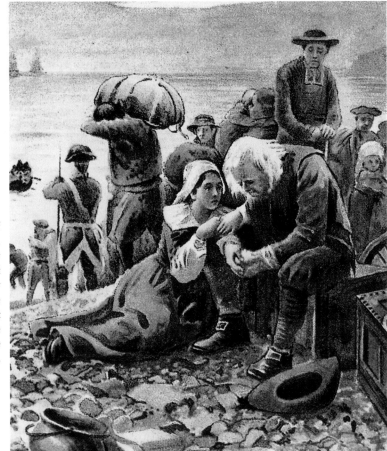

An artist's view of the expulsion. Having hastily packed what possessions they can carry, the despondent Acadians await the ship that will take them into exile.

If many people today remember the Acadians' tragic fate, it is probably thanks to a poem written about 100 years after the deportation by an American poet, Henry Wadsworth Longfellow. "Evangeline" tells the sad story of the young Acadian lovers Evangeline and Gabriel, engaged to be married when the deportation wrenches them apart. The poem powerfully evokes the finality of the Acadians' loss as they watch their farms burn:

> Columns of shining smoke uprose, and flashes of flame
> were
> Thrust through their folds and withdrawn like the
> quivering hands of a martyr. . . .
> These things beheld in dismay the crowd
> on the shore and on shipboard.
> Speechless at first they stood, then cried aloud
> in their anguish,
> "We shall behold no more our homes in the village
> of Grand-Pré!"

Although many modern Acadians reject the image Longfellow created of the Acadian as a passive victim, the poem took on legendary status. It was read by schoolchildren, printed in newspapers, and recited at rallies. The poem bound the community together as nothing beside their religion had done. Prominent nineteenth-century lawyer Pascal Poirier recalled carrying a copy of "Evangeline" close to his heart in his student days at the Collège St-Joseph, where he would declaim entire passages aloud during long walks.

Once the peace treaty between France and Britain was signed in 1763, the British allowed the Acadians to return, although not to their old land, much of which had been settled by New Englanders and settlers from Yorkshire, England. From as far away as France, many returned. Some filtered back over the Quebec border; some got land in the Memramcook area (southeast of Moncton), along the upper Saint John River valley, or on the North Shore, where they engaged in fishing and some farming.

# CHAPTER 4

# From the Loyalists to 1900

**B**ecause many families have lived in New Brunswick for generations, it is easy to forget that all New Brunswickers, with the exception of the Micmacs and Maliseets, are descended from immigrants. The ancestors of many New Brunswickers immigrated in the late eighteenth century.

New immigration began shortly after the deportation of the Acadians. The British wanted the land to be settled and tilled. They tried to interest some of the soldiers who had organized the expulsion of the Acadians in staying and farming, and also encouraged settlers from New England, where fertile land was becoming scarce, to move north. Massachusetts settlers established Sackville on the Chignecto Isthmus and Maugerville, in the Saint John River valley; farmers from Yorkshire, England, also came to Chignecto. After 1764, when the Acadians were allowed to return, some came from Pennsylvania to the Memramcook valley, and others worked at fishing stations run by Charles Robin around Caraquet, on the Bay of Chaleur. Scottish fishermen settled on the Miramichi, Nepisiguit and Restigouche rivers, and six German families from Pennsylvania landed in 1763 on the Petitcodiac.

But the biggest wave, by far, was the American Loyalists. Terrible things were happening to people who had remained loyal to the British Crown during the American Revolution. Roving mobs calling themselves the "Sons of Liberty" burned people's barns and livestock and tarred and feathered Loyalists. Their

The mill at Stanley, 1835. In the early 1800s, most New Brunswick wood was exported as squared timber. By the mid 1820s, however, sawmills were multiplying and producing vast amounts of sawn lumber for use by local shipbuilders as well as for export.

The first shiploads of Loyalists arrive at the mouth of the Saint John River, May 18, 1783.

property was confiscated, and those convicted of treason might be hanged publicly. Fearing for their safety, 100 000 left. About 40 000 went to Nova Scotia, which at that time included New Brunswick. To this day, the citizens of Saint John designate the third week in July as Loyalist Days, although the actual date of the Loyalist landing at the mouth of the Saint John River was May 18, 1783.

The Loyalists encompassed a cross-section of colonial society, including wealthy businessmen, farmers, artisans and tradesmen, from Massachusetts, New York, New Jersey and Connecticut. There were also several thousand Blacks, of whom about 1000 settled in the future province of New Brunswick. Some had fought with the Loyalist armies in exchange for their freedom; others were slaves of wealthy Loyalists.

The first sight of Parr Town (Saint John), a small trading post in scrubby wilderness, must have been disenchanting for people used to the bustling cities of Boston and New York. One woman wrote in her diary: "I climbed to the top of Chipman's Hill and watched the sails disappear, and such a lonely feeling came over me that, although I had not shed a tear through all the war, I sat down on the damp moss with my baby in my lap and cried."

The first winter was especially hard. While some were lucky enough to complete one-room log cabins, late arrivals spent it in tents thatched with spruce boughs and banked with snow. Some died of cold and malnutrition.

By the end of the century, however, the Loyalists had prospered. A young Englishman who arrived in Saint John to build ships was surprised to find a city "uncommonly orderly and well conducted," with women "remarkably well dressed, clean, neat and affecting a degree of fashionability surprising in such a place."

At Sainte-Anne in the Saint John River valley, arriving Loyalists with land titles evicted an established settlement of Acadian refugees from the deportation. The Acadians' leader, Louis Mercure, petitioned for land far up the valley. Together with Acadian settlers displaced from the Kennebecasis valley, this group formed the core of the Madawaska Acadian community.

## Displacement of Native Peoples

All of these settlements violated a 1763 Royal proclamation making it illegal to settle Native peoples' lands without their consent. Nor had the Micmacs or Maliseets surrendered any of their land in earlier peace treaties with the colonial authorities.

Yet when problems arose between Natives and Loyalists on the Miramichi and Richibucto rivers in 1788, Governor Thomas Carleton excluded Natives from the village of Richibucto. Friction also arose on the Saint John River following the massive influx of Loyalists, who dispossessed Maliseets as far north as what is now Woodstock. Even the site of the main Maliseet village at Ekw-pa-hakw was fraudulently expropriated for the benefit of a prominent Loyalist.

Dispersed, outnumbered, and ravaged by European diseases such as smallpox and typhus, Micmacs and Maliseets were increasingly restricted to reserve lands. Denied freedom of movement and access to the fish and game that had sustained them for centuries, they regularly faced cold and starvation. Nor did the situation improve

With the coming of the Loyalists, the Micmacs and Maliseets were displaced from the lands they had occupied for centuries. They soon found themselves restricted to ever more marginal areas where it became harder and harder for them to follow their traditional hunting and fishing way of life.

with time.  By 1844 the New Brunswick legislature had passed a law permitting the sale of the remaining reserve land, much of which passed into the hands of non-Natives.

## A New Colony

To the frustration of the Loyalist settlers, the affairs of the colony were run long-distance, by the governor in Halifax. They petitioned for more local control, and in 1784 the colony of "New Brunswick" was partitioned from Nova Scotia.  The name recognized King George III's roots in the German duchy of Brunswick-Lunenburg. Since Saint John had a reputation for commercialism and rowdiness, the capital was moved to Fredericton, which to this day maintains a more genteel atmosphere than the port city.

## Economic Growth

The colony grew enormously over the next half-century.  From 25 000 citizens, the population soared to 200 000 by mid-century, and the economy surged.

The Napoleonic Wars in Europe and the War of 1812 in North America provided the necessary boost.  There was money to be made

Felling and hauling logs. Trees were felled in winter, both because they were easier to cut down when the sap wasn't running and because the snow made them easier to haul to the riverside. After the ice broke up in spring, they were dumped into the water and floated downstream to the mills.

This 1834 picture of the process of clearing the townsite at Stanley illustrates the difficulties that awaited settlers as they spread across the province.

*privateering* — capturing enemy (that is, American, or "Yankee") ships and confiscating their cargoes. To fight the war at sea, the British Navy needed wooden ships, but Napoleon had cut off their Baltic timber supply, so they turned to the timber in New Brunswick forests. Logging boomed, as did wooden shipbuilding along New Brunswick's coasts and rivers.

By the 1830s, New Brunswick ships had earned a reputation for construction and design, and by mid-century New Brunswick shipyards were building over 100 ships a year. Scottish immigrants established two of the biggest firms — Alexander Rankin and James Gilmour's at Douglastown, and James Fraser's on Beaubear's Island. Another Scot, Joseph Russell, took over and expanded the capacity of the Fraser firm to allow work on five ships simultaneously. Their chief competitor was the flamboyant Joseph Cunard of Halifax (brother of steamship magnate Samuel). His mills and shipbuilding operations on the Miramichi, in Bathurst and in Kouchibouguac employed hundreds of men until his business failed in 1847. It is said that he faced down an angry mob of workers with a pistol in each boot and the challenge, "Now let's see the man who would shoot Cunard!"

Most renowned of the New Brunswick ships was the clipper *Marco Polo*. Under her fanatical skipper Bully Forbes she outraced the steam packet *Australia* to Melbourne in 1851, making the return voyage in just under six months when eight or nine was considered good time for a windjammer.

## More Newcomers

From the War of 1812 until mid-century, cheap labour poured in from the British Isles to farm, work the forests and build the ships. There was a Welsh settlement at Cardigan, north of Fredericton. Irish Protestants settled in the lower Saint John River valley, where they blended in with the rest of the Protestant population. The Irish Catholics, who often did not speak English, were generally poorer; they settled along the Miramichi River and in Saint John.

The nature of the Irish immigrants and their reception varied. Small farmers with capital, tradesmen and skilled artisans were often well received, but others arrived sick and destitute. Between

By 1851, Saint John had a population of 22 745 and was still growing.

1846 and 1849, the potato crop of Ireland was struck by a blight. During this great Potato Famine, thousands of poor Irish immigrants arrived weak from hunger or disease. Their boats were known as "fever ships," and in 1847 more than 2000 died of typhus en route. Others died on Middle Island, a quarantine site on the Miramichi River, and in the Poor House hospital in Saint John; you can still see the Celtic crosses in their cemeteries.

These new arrivals were not welcomed by Protestant New Brunswickers, who saw them as cheap competition for jobs, and associated them with laziness, crime and alcohol. Indeed, crime and rowdiness accompanied their squalid living conditions; the crowded tenements of York Point in Saint John had no outdoor privy, and Flagor Alley was closed to habitation after a cholera epidemic in 1854.

Fearing the growth of the Irish Catholic population, Irish Protestants formed a New Brunswick branch of the Loyal Orange Order, which grew into a politically influential organization of Protestants loyal to the British Crown and fearful of Irish and French Catholic growth. Riots erupted between Orange Order supporters and Catholics throughout the 1840s, culminating in the 1849 riot in Saint John, which left at least 12 dead. Tension gradually diminished with a decline in Irish immigration and the absorption of the children of new immigrants into the New Brunswick mainstream.

Of all the immigrant groups to New Brunswick, the Irish were the most important. Between 1815 and 1865, at least 66 percent of all New Brunswick immigrants, most of whom landed at Saint John, St. Andrews and the Miramichi, were Irish. By 1851, 45 percent of the heads of household in Fredericton were Irish-born; in "Loyalist" Saint John, they formed a majority.

The province could not have been built without them. Irish labour developed the lumber industry, built the railways, and worked the mills, shipyards and factories. Many farmed successfully, settling Johnville in Carleton County, at Grand Lake near the Canaan River, and near Salisbury in Westmorland County.

By the second half of the nineteenth century, Irish Catholics were representing their constituencies in the House of Assembly, starting with Martin Cranney for Northumberland County in 1846. The second and third generations opened businesses and entered the professions. And New Brunswick culture is richer for the folktales and folksongs of the logging camps of the Miramichi, including Michael Whalen's "Dungarvon Whooper," the tale of a logger whose howling ghost continues to haunt the river.

The War of 1812 also brought many runaway Black slaves, dispatched by the British from the United States to Nova Scotia. The New Brunswick government reluctantly accepted about 500. Settled without financial support, provisions or farm implements on stony land at Loch Lomond (near Saint John), they were refused

*Top right: Soldiers' Barracks at Fredericton, Winter 1834.* **After Fredericton was chosen as the capital and military headquarters of the new province, British officers became the centre of the town's lively social scene.**
*Bottom right:* **Bathurst in the mid-1800s. The town was built around the end of the seventeenth century on the site of an early French settlement established by Nicholas Denys.**

clear title to their small lots (half the size of white settlers' holdings). A rare friend was Judge Ward Chipman, who called it "a cruel thing that they should have been sent by government to this . . . inhospitable climate, and left without any aid in making a settlement." Over the years, their lots passed into white hands.

In the 1870s, Danes arrived to farm in Victoria County, near today's New Denmark. Scottish farmers, whose agricultural techniques were regarded as quite progressive, settled along the Saint John River in Victoria County, where names like Kintore and Kincardine reflect their founders' heritage.

## Confederation and Its Aftermath

New Brunswick's geographical position made it indispensable to any union of the British North American colonies, but few people in the province showed much interest when the idea of Confederation was first proposed in 1864. The New Brunswick economy looked eastward to Britain, or south to New England, not westward across the continent.

What changed people's minds? One factor was the prospect of a railway linking the province to central Canada. This would expand trade to the west at the expense of the United States, which had threatened to end the Reciprocity Treaty (and did, in 1866). Defence also entered the picture. A railway would make it easier to move troops along the U.S. border, at a time when relations with the young republic were not always as friendly as they are today.

The first New Brunswick election fought over Confederation, in February and March of 1865, saw the Confederates, under Leonard Tilley, roundly defeated by Albert Smith's "antis." A year later, however, the noisy threats and occasional violence of the Fenians, a band of anti-British, pro-Irish nationalists massed on the Maine-New Brunswick border, set the stage for a pro-Confederation vote. In a campaign that labelled French and Irish Catholics, many of whom opposed Confederation, disloyal to the British crown,

*Top right:* The little tramp steamer in this painting (entitled *The Tramp*) forecasts the end of the age of wooden sailing ships and the beginning of the age of iron hulls and steam.

*Bottom right:* The Intercolonial Railway was finally completed in 1876. Seen here in the Moncton yards shortly afterwards are some of the people involved in running it and express locomotive 66.

Tilley's Confederates won overwhelmingly. By June, 1866, New Brunswick was squarely behind Confederation.

The immediate consequences of Confederation were good for New Brunswick. The Intercolonial Railway linked the province with central Canada in 1876, and freight rates from central Canada to the Maritimes were kept low. Prime Minister John A. Macdonald's National Policy favoured the growth of Maritime industries; it kept duties low on imported raw materials like cotton and hemp, while protecting manufactured goods. In the 1880s, cities like Moncton, a railway centre, and ports like Saint John and St. Stephen boomed. The value of Saint John's industrial output increased by 98 percent in the decade, and the city became Canada's leading producer of nails and brass. A large cotton mill near Fredericton thrived, and the development of steamships meant that New Brunswick potatoes arrived quickly in the West Indies.

The 1880s were a time of political maturation and consolidation.

Until Andrew Blair's premiership (1883-1896) New Brunswick's party system was weak. Since politicians were not loyal to a particular party, it was easy to corrupt them. A visitor to the province wrote in 1884, "The price of a New Brunswick politician ranges from two or three thousand dollars down to probably a hundred dollars, and his rule of disposal is to go to whoever gives him the highest price." Blair, however, built a strong Liberal Party by insisting that his members vote the party line. He also abolished the Legislative Council (the Upper House), and did away with property qualifications for members of the legislature.

Towards the end of the century, wooden shipbuilding, the linchpin of the New Brunswick economy, went into decline. As iron steamships proved their worth, the 1880s saw the end of the "Golden Age of Sail." New Brunswickers lost their jobs in logging and shipbuilding, and many left the province to work in New England, known as the "Boston States," to find work.

Many shipbuilders invested in other industries, such as iron foundries and textile mills. But by 1900, industrial decline had begun, as businesses failed or were bought out by national chains in central Canada.

## Confederation and Native People

For Micmacs and Maliseets, the birth of Canada brought little improvement. Shortly after Confederation, the new Parliament passed the Indian Act, which would control nearly every aspect of Native life in Canada. In its attempt to assimilate Natives to the Canadian way of life, it damaged the fibre of Native culture. Under the Act's provisions for education, for example, generations of Native children were removed from their families and communities to residential schools, where they were taught to forget their own culture and language, and were often abused. Many new Brunswick Native children were sent to the residential school in Shubenacadie, Nova Scotia, which did not close until the 1960s.

# CHAPTER 5

# The Acadians: Renaissance and Resurgence

**F**or about a century after the deportation, the Acadians remained a poor, uneducated and powerless people. They were not involved in government or in the debate over entering Confederation.

For this to change, they needed leaders who could represent their community within the government. This was made possible with the founding of the Collège St-Joseph at Memramcook in 1864. In the years that followed, this institution would graduate Acadian lawyers, teachers and politicians.

The Acadian community also needed a forum where they could publicly debate their concerns. Today, this might mean a French-language television or radio station, but in 1867 it meant a newspaper. The first French newspaper, the *Moniteur Acadien,* was founded in 1867. Two more followed over the next two decades.

Initially, Acadians had only token representation in the Legislative Assembly, beginning with the election of Amand Landry in 1846. He was to be the sole Acadian member until 1866, when Vital Hébert was elected from Victoria-Madawaska.

It was not uncommon in the nineteenth century for Acadians to encounter bigotry, both inside and outside the legislature. Once, an English member accused Acadians of having a disproportionate number of insane people in the asylum. Thinking fast, Acadian MLA Urbain Johnson shot back that the Acadians sent their "idiots" to the asylums, while the English sent them to the legislature!

In mid-August 1994, the Acadians of southeastern New Brunswick hosted the first Congrès Mondial Acadien (Acadian World Congress). By the tens of thousands, descendants of Acadians deported in the 1750s came from across Canada, from Louisiana and other American states, from Britain and France to celebrate their roots and their cultural survival.

What finally awakened the mass of Acadians politically, however, was an issue that touched many of them personally — Premier George King's Common Schools Act of 1870.

To modern ears, this was a progressive piece of legislation; the government wanted to establish a non-religious system of public schools financed by taxes. This meant that schooling would be available to all children, not just to those whose parents could afford to pay. At the time, many Acadians were poor fishermen and loggers with large families, and only 20 percent of their children attended school. Those who did go to school went to religious institutions, with priests and nuns as teachers. Under the government's bill, this would have to change. The Acadians liked their religious schools, and resisted.

Anti-Catholic rhetoric characterized the 1874 election, which King's Conservatives won resoundingly on a pro-Schools Act platform. But the collection of the new school tax energized the Acadians as nothing had before.

The "Caraquet Riots" of January 1875. The death of Constable Gifford, depicted here, and of Louis Mailloux shocked the government into finding an alternative to the public school law that had so outraged the Acadians.

The conflict came to a head in Caraquet in 1875. The so-called "Caraquet Riots" were tame indeed; they were gatherings of Acadian men angered at the refusal of the authorities to seat Acadians who had boycotted the school taxes on the school board. Sadly, what began as an attempt to arrest the ringleaders of these sometimes rowdy mobs ended with the deaths of one Acadian, Louis Mailloux, and one of the men called up to enforce the government policy, John Gifford.

This tragic turn of events finally convinced the government that compromise was in order. Although schools would remain state-supported, nuns and priests were permitted to teach in their traditional habits, anti-Catholic bias was to be removed from textbooks, convents could be leased to schoolboards, and there would be no restrictions on the use of schools after school hours.

## Acadian Women

The role of Acadian women during this period is often overlooked. Throughout the nineteenth and the first half of the twentieth centuries, the contribution of married women to the community

The graduating class of the Bouctouche Convent, c. 1952

was typically restricted to the home. The case was substantially different, however, for Acadian women in religious orders. Initially, their convents were organized by women from Quebec or France, but local talent developed quickly.

By the mid-nineteenth century, various orders of nuns had opened schools for girls in Tracadie, Caraquet and Saint-Louis de Kent. By the 1920s, convents had opened in other parishes, educating Acadian girls and turning out a good proportion of the local teachers, many bilingual. The first colleges for women were also established by religious orders, including the Collège Notre-Dame d'Acadie, founded in Memramcook in 1943.

The convents doubled as community cultural centres where art and music classes were offered. Acadia's first hospitals, including the leper hospital established in Tracadie in 1868, were founded and administered by nuns.

## The Acadian Renaissance

Acadian self-renewal crystallized in a series of Acadian congresses, beginning with the one held in Memramcook on July 21-22, 1881, and attended by thousands of Maritime Acadians. The result was a national organization, the Société Nationale l'Assomption, a hymn, "Ave Maris Stella," and a national day, the Feast of the Assumption, August 15. Later would come a flag, the French tricolour with the star of Mary. Out of these congresses sprang Acadian leaders from among the elite, mostly from Southern New Brunswick.

Over the past century, New Brunswick's Acadians have gradually come of age, in part through population growth. In 1871, 16 percent of New Brunswickers claimed French ancestry; this rose to 24 percent by 1901 and to almost 40 percent by 1961. Assimilation into the English-speaking majority is, however, of perpetual concern to the Acadian minority. In the 1961 census, 35 percent of New Brunswickers declared themselves French-speaking; this was slightly down, to 33 percent, by 1991.

The Moncton campus of the Université de Moncton. The university also has campuses at Edmundston and Shippagan.

The growth of local French educational institutions, however, has produced a dynamic group of leaders. Since World War II, the number of Acadian MLAs has reflected their proportion in the population, and since 1878, New Brunswick Acadians have been represented by at least three Members of Parliament in Ottawa.

In 1923, Peter Veniot became the first Acadian premier of New Brunswick when Walter Foster stepped down. Veniot raised the political profile of Acadians, cementing their attachment to the Liberal Party by campaigning against conscription in 1917 and spending heavily on public works in Acadian constituencies. Following his two-year premiership, he became the first New Brunswick Acadian in the federal cabinet.

The first Acadian to become premier as the result of an election was Louis J. Robichaud, who governed New Brunswick for the Liberal Party from 1960 to 1970. Robichaud's legislation supporting the economic and linguistic equality of French and English in New Brunswick signalled a marked improvement in Acadian status.

The ripple effect of the Université de Moncton, founded under the Robichaud government in 1963, has been astounding: a flourishing study of Acadian literature and language, an art gallery, an educated class of bilingual business people, educators, civil servants, lawyers and engineers.

Acadian-run businesses are increasingly common, including Assumption Mutual Life Insurance Company (Assomption Compagnie Mutuelle d'Assurance-Vie), which began in 1903 as the Société de l'Assomption, collecting a small sum for health and life insurance from Acadians who went to work in the New England cotton and shoe factories. It is now a major life insurance company and an important investor in the region. The Pizza Delight chain, which began as the class project of two Université de Moncton business students in the late 1960s, now has over 150 Canadian franchises and has expanded to the United Arab Emirates. More recently, telecommunications and information-based companies have been attracted to New Brunswick in part because of the many educated Acadians who are fluent in both French and English.

## French Language Rights

None of this occurred without resentment from some segments of the New Brunswick population. The "Official Languages of New Brunswick Act," which guaranteed the equality of French and English in all government institutions, was enacted in the legislature under Premier Robichaud on September 1, 1969. Yet in Moncton as late as 1972, the City Council under Mayor Leonard Jones refused to appoint a committee to study the implementation of bilingual city services.

But gradually things began to change. Federal Conservative leader Robert Stanfield rejected Jones as a Conservative candidate in the 1974 federal election because of his stand on bilingualism. By 1977, Moncton City Hall had instituted bilingual switchboard service and committed itself to bilingual services.

Conservative premier Richard Hatfield continued his Liberal predecessor's commitment to bilingualism, both at the provincial and national levels. With Bill 88 in 1981, his government explicitly recognized the rights of both language communities, garnering an unprecedented amount of support for the Conservative party from the Acadian community as a result. And his Liberal successor, Frank McKenna, entrenched the collective rights of both communities to their distinct educational and cultural institutions in the federal Constitution in 1992.

There is periodic dissension over language and culture within the Acadian community. Acadians in the north sometimes feel that the southeastern Acadians have too much control. The Parti Acadien, now defunct, talked of forming a separate Acadian province, and some Acadians have favoured joining Quebec. But by and large Acadian opinion favours the strengthening of their community within a bilingual province. And since 1960 New Brunswick governments, of both major parties, have demonstrated that they will promote the French language and culture.

**Boat decorated for the Blessing of the Fleet, an enduring tradition at Acadian fishing ports. *Inset:* The Acadian Historical Village at Caraquet recreates the way of life of the Acadians who established themselves in the area in the late 1700s.**

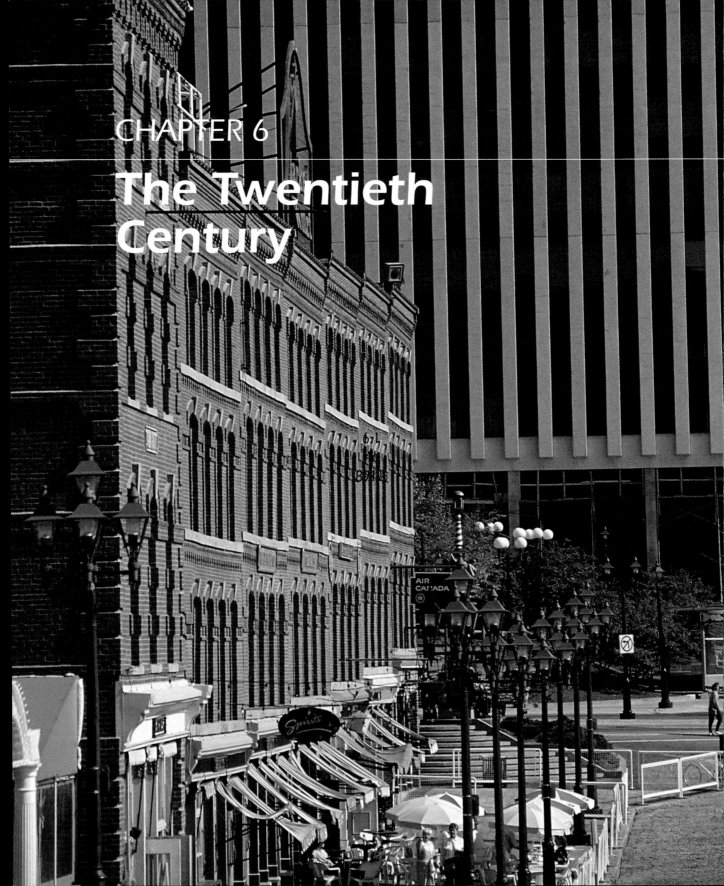

# CHAPTER 6

# The Twentieth
# Century

Canada's role in the First World War, especially the victory at Vimy Ridge, strengthened its sense of nationhood. The war also gave a strong boost to the flagging New Brunswick economy. Industry expanded to meet wartime demand, and the port of Saint John, fortified for the war's duration, was extremely active.

The war received strong support among English New Brunswickers. The province's infantry unit, the 26th Battalion, was composed of men from across the province — Saint John and the Upper Valley, the Tantramar, the Miramichi, and the French North Shore. Known as "the Fighting 26th," it saw action in most of the major battles of the Western Front — Ypres, Arras, Vimy Ridge, Passchendaele, Cambrai. At the Somme, the 26th took 600 German prisoners, more than its total strength, at a cost of two-thirds of its men. Back home, the Saint John community raised funds for a field kitchen, for a Christmas dinner in 1916, and for pipers. By war's end, the battalion had garnered 334 honours and awards.

Col. L. C. Daigle mounted a strong enlistment effort among Acadians for the 165th Acadian Battalion. As in the rest of French Canada, however, identification with a war for British Imperial interests was weak, and Acadian public opinion objected to conscription. As the number of French names on cenotaphs throughout the province attests, many Acadians gave their lives in this war and the next. Still, Acadian resistance to forced service aroused a resentment in English New Brunswick that still lingers in some segments of the population.

**The Saint John waterfront underwent a major transformation in the 1980s. Here, the nineteenth-century facades of Market Square provide a contrast to sleek new highrises.**

In 1919, the New Brunswick government recognized the enormous contribution of the province's women to the war effort at home and overseas by awarding them the vote. Although women had been active from the mid-nineteenth-century in New Brunswick's temperance movement, the women's suffrage movement was not strong in the province, as it had been in the West. Women would not be entitled to run for provincial office until 1934.

## Hard Times

With the end of the war, industry went into a slump. New Brunswickers continued to leave the province in the 1920s as fishing, lumbering, sawmilling and farming declined. Farms themselves got larger, but their actual number dropped by 6 percent in the decade, as more and more people living in the country went into other work. Increasingly, people living on the land took temporary jobs in fishing, logging and construction.

A farmers' protest movement, United Farmers, grew up in the 1920s. It was particularly strong in the potato belt along the upper Saint John River valley, where farmers wanted favourable prices for their potato exports. United Farmers ran candidates in the 1920 election, winning 21 percent of the votes and 11 seats. It also developed a network of co-operatives, the United Farmers Co-operative Company of New Brunswick, which by 1920 had opened 23 local stores. Although the United Farmers did not last as a political party, it had an impact on the government as a lobby for farm interests.

Although the lumber trade fell off, one bright area in the 1920s was pulp and paper. Pulpwood production more than doubled in the decade, with pulp mills opening in Bathurst and Edmundston, and a newsprint plant opening in Dalhousie. It is a sign of the changes in the New Brunswick economy that by the end of the decade, about one in four farmers and fishermen was working in the woods for some part of the year.

*Top:* Unemployed workers planting garden plots in 1932 with seed and fertilizer supplied by the Rotary Club. *Bottom:* Second-hand store in one of Saint John's poorer neighbourhoods in the 1920s

The 1920s was also a time for increased spending on public works. As a cabinet minister under Walter Foster and later as premier, Peter Veniot left an important legacy: the New Brunswick Electric Power Commission, the Grand Falls hydroelectric plant, and a highway system to accommodate the growing number of cars.

Just as Confederation had been credited for the mid-century railway and industrial boom, now it was blamed for hard times. Delegates of the new Maritime Rights Movement representing local boards of trade and professionals went to Ottawa in 1925 with their grievances. The government responded with the Duncan Commission, whose report recommended many economic adjustments to favour the Maritime economy. The result was the Maritime Freight Rates Act, offering favourable freight rates for goods exported from the Maritimes to central Canada, and Harbour Boards for Halifax and Saint John.

Many of the commission's recommendations were interpreted restrictively or ignored, however, and the Great Depression of the 1930s hit the Maritimes harder than any region east of the Prairies. Since it was continent-wide, this time Maritimers could not go "down the road" to the "Boston States" for work.

Social assistance was a local responsibility, but without healthy businesses to sustain them many counties simply did not have the money to finance their enormous relief roles. There were even reports of starvation. A telegram from the Northumberland County Council to Prime Minister R. B. Bennett read, "Large numbers destitute to danger of starvation." Since hungry people were more susceptible to disease, tuberculosis was rife in the north.

New Brunswickers did not react passively to the Depression; many organized to help themselves. In the fisheries, Father Livain Chiasson of Shippagan, who had been influenced by Nova Scotia's innovative Antigonish Movement, helped to organize the United Maritime Fishermen, which by 1938 had developed co-operative stores, lobster canneries, fish-processing plants and credit unions. In the Miramichi, the Farmer-Labour Union of farmers, woodworkers and longshoremen organized study clubs, co-operatives and credit unions to encourage local processing and give labourers a greater share in profits. Nor was the government of Premier Alison Dysart unresponsive to workers' pressures. It appointed a Fair Wage Officer and Board, moved to have lumber companies give up unexploited forest land, and passed the New Brunswick Labour Bill guaranteeing workers the right to form and join unions without penalty.

The Second World War put an end to the Depression. Unemployment ended, with many men overseas or involved in war production in central Canada. There was a need for skilled artisans; in cities like Halifax and Saint John, suddenly there was a shortage of workers. With the St. Lawrence River less secure from German

Soldiers of New Brunswick's Carleton and York Regiment make their way through a street in southern Italy as part of the Allied advance towards Rome during the Second World War.

submarines, traffic at Saint John increased, and shipyards were kept busy repairing vessels damaged in the Battle of the Atlantic.

Overseas, New Brunswickers served with distinction. The North Shore Regiment fought valiantly in Normandy and in the Netherlands campaign, which their historian described as "a misery they had not known before . . . taking desperate chances, probing, fleeing, trying to outguess the enemy."

When the war was over, so was the economic boom. A postwar study indicated that the province had the highest rate of infant mortality (death of babies under a year of age) in Canada and the highest illiteracy rate. New Brunswick spent just slightly more than half the national average on education and health. It was clear that the province was ripe for a change, one that would close the gap between it and the rest of Canada.

## Moving New Brunswick Ahead

Postwar New Brunswick saw three premiers in succession determined to make this change.

Of these, Louis J. Robichaud had the most dramatic impact, altering the face of the province in a decade (1960-1970) as it had not been altered in a century. The energy of "Little Louis" or "P'tit Louis," as he was affectionately nicknamed for his short stature,

57

belied his size.  Measuring all of 165 cm (five feet five inches), he was a dynamo.

Through his "Program of Equal Opportunity," Robichaud was determined to rectify the enormous disparities in health, wealth and education between northern and southern, French and English, and rural and urban New Brunswick. He restructured the government to eliminate the county councils.  He gave the provincial government control over education, social assistance and medical and judicial services, leaving only property services (water, sewer and policing) to the municipalities.  Government grew, but poorer, usually rural, communities finally had hospitals and high schools.  Robichaud also boosted the status of Acadians.  He passed the first legislation for bilingualism, increased the number of Acadians employed in the civil service and established the Université de Moncton.

Richard B. Hatfield's Conservative  government (1970-1987) continued to expand the government's role in the economy.  And Hatfield reached out, as no Conservative premier had before, to the Acadian community.  To counteract the assimilation of French by

The great dam at Mactaquac, near Fredericton, was built in the 1960s. The first four units of the hydroelectric station — the largest in the Maritimes — went into operation in 1968, and two more were added later.

English, he replaced bilingual schools by two parallel school systems, one French and one English. His Bill 88, introduced in 1981, broadened the scope of official bilingualism from equality of government services to the equality of the two linguistic communities. In the 1982 provincial election, the Conservative landslide included unprecedented electoral support from French New Brunswickers.

The Hatfield years were plagued with mismanagement and personal scandal — from allegations of kickbacks to an estimated $25 million of government money down the drain for a Bricklin sports car factory that never went into large-scale production. Yet Hatfield's legacy includes important reform legislation — stricter government tendering procedures, fairer civil service hiring, increased public access to government information, and limits on corporate and individual contributions to political parties.

Upon Hatfield's death from brain cancer at the age of 60, one writer called the ex-premier "a splash of colour in the grey world of Canadian politics." Nicknamed "Disco Dick" for his free-spirited lifestyle, he was an atypical politician — a bachelor who

A trend towards larger but fewer farms has meant that abandoned farms like this one, at McGowan's Corner on the Saint John River, have become a fairly common sight in recent decades.

Premier Frank McKenna (left) takes time out from the heavier burdens of office to participate in the 1994 Miramichi Irish Festival.

supported fine crafts and had a private collection of antique dolls. The president of the Université de Moncton remembered him with gratitude: "We always felt that he supported the Acadian population and the university, that he understood our aspirations, and that he was proud of our accomplishments."

Premier Frank McKenna, first elected in the Liberal clean sweep of 1987, has emphasized the connection between the provincial economy and education. The government has tried to reduce the provincial deficit by amalgamating municipal services and school and hospital boards, and by welfare reform. To attract business to the province, McKenna has travelled extensively in Canada, the United States and Asia, emphasizing the province's bilingual work force. The government has emphasized the use of standardized testing and required more math and science courses in New Brunswick schools.

## Native People

If New Brunswick was economically backward in relation to the rest of Canada in the postwar period, the Micmacs and Maliseets were

*Left:* **Micmac youngsters at the Red Bank Metepenagiag Federal School learn to drum from their elders.** *Right:* **Constable Trevor Bear, one of seven Native policemen on the Tobique First Nation Reserve. Legislation giving the reserve police more responsibility was passed recently.**

particularly disadvantaged in their education, health and living conditions. Jobs were scarce, reserves lacked electricity, sewers and good roads, and malnutrition and tuberculosis were common.

During the late 1960s, Native bands formed the Union of New Brunswick Indians to deal with such issues and with land claims and other aboriginal and treaty rights. In the decades that followed, the University of New Brunswick began training Micmacs and Maliseets as teachers, and Saint Thomas University introduced a Native studies program, the only one east of Montreal.

While Native people are still controlled by the Indian Act, there is pressure now throughout Canada to abolish it. In the meantime, New Brunswick Native communities and organizations are working hard to liberate themselves from the dependency the Act fosters. Some look for solutions in non-Native governmental structures and in projects to generate economic development, like the Micmac Maliseet Development Corporation on the Eel Ground Reserve. Others are revitalizing the traditional spiritual, economic, social and political systems which have sustained their people for millennia.

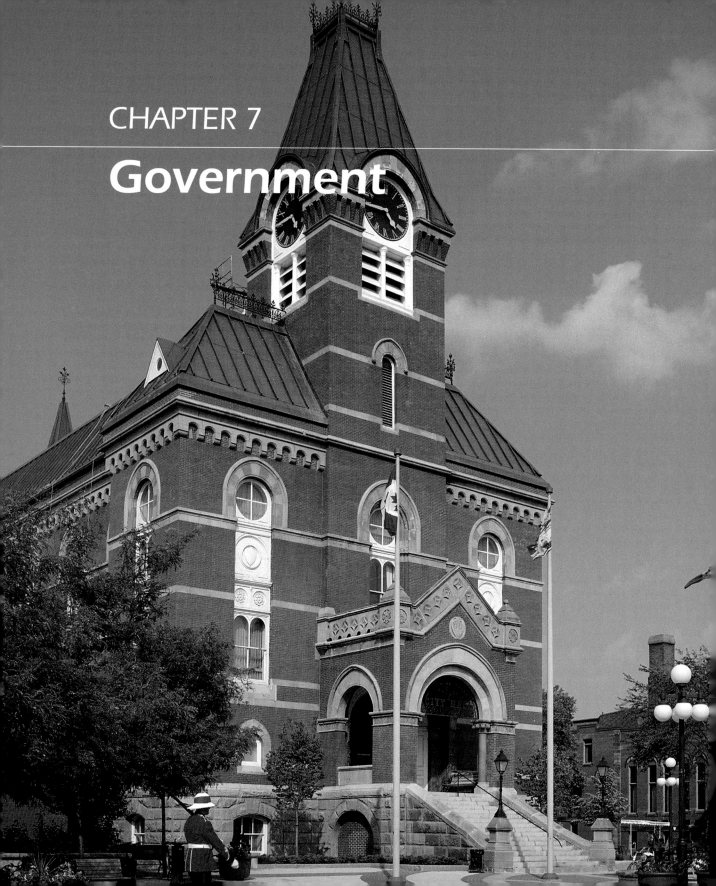

CHAPTER 7

# Government

**G**overnment has changed enormously since New Brunswick became a separate colony in 1784. At that time, the province was governed like other British colonies — by an appointed lieutenant-governor and a Legislative Council selected from the wealthier classes of society. The elected House of Assembly had a broader population base but less power.

In the 1840s many people in Upper Canada and Nova Scotia were demanding *responsible government,* that is, government that held power only so long as it had the support of the majority of the people's elected representatives. New Brunswick had its share of reformers agitating for a more democratic, less colonial form of government, though none with the eloquence or popular support of Nova Scotia's Joseph Howe. The British government finally granted responsible government to Nova Scotia and Upper Canada in 1848, and to a somewhat reluctant New Brunswick six years later. Today, the only vestige of colonial government is the lieutenant-governor, who represents the Queen in largely ceremonial duties — reading the Speech from the Throne, giving "Royal Assent" to legislation and presiding over special functions in the Queen's name.

A government is formed by the political party that can command a majority of the 58 seats in the Legislative Assembly. The leader of that party becomes the premier and appoints a cabinet whose members, called ministers, head government departments, such as Health and Community Services, Finance or Education.

A lone sentry patrols in front of Fredericton's City Hall, the oldest city hall still in use in the Maritimes. The clock in the tower still is wound by hand.

New Brunswick's stately Legislative Building and the chamber where the 58-seat assembly meets

Elections must be held every five years, but they may also be called if the government is defeated on a vote of confidence on a major piece of legislation.

At the federal level, New Brunswick has ten seats in the House of Commons. Traditionally, the province has had at least one cabinet minister. The province is guaranteed ten Senate seats by the Constitution.

## Courts

The highest court in New Brunswick is the Supreme Court. It has two divisions — the Court of Queen's Bench and the Court of Appeals. The Court of Queen's Bench has a trial division, which hears criminal and civil cases, and a family division, which handles such issues as divorce and child custody. Cases are heard by a judge and sometimes a jury, and verdicts can be appealed to the Court of Appeals. Another level of court is the Provincial Court, which handles only criminal matters and is also responsible for cases involving young offenders, aged 12 to 18.

## Medical Care

In Canada, medical care is a provincial responsibility supported by federal taxes. About 22 percent of health care in New Brunswick is federally funded. All eligible New Brunswickers are covered by the provincial medical insurance plan, New Brunswick Medicare, which covers hospital care and doctors' fees. The increasing expense of this service has prompted the province to develop cost-saving measures. The number of hospital boards has been reduced and home care has been expanded to shorten hospital stays. Another provincial service is Public Health, which immunizes babies and young children, screens children for vision and hearing problems and provides an in-school fluoride program. The province sets standards for nursing homes for senior citizens and covers the cost of prescription drugs for some people.

## Education

New Brunswick has two parallel school systems, one English and one French. French immersion education for English-speaking children is widely available, and New Brunswick has the highest rate of enrollment in French immersion of any province. A full-day public kindergarten program was introduced in 1991.

The province has four universities: the University of New Brunswick (UNB), St. Thomas University in Fredericton, Mount Allison in Sackville and Université de Moncton. UNB has campuses in Fredericton and Saint John, and Université de Moncton has campuses at Moncton, Edmundston and Shippagan. There are nine

*Left:* The arts building of the University of New Brunswick in Fredericton is the oldest university building in Canada. *Right:* Mount Allison University's Convocation Hall, Sackville. Mount Allison was the first Canadian university to grant a Bachelor of Fine Arts degree and the first in the British Empire to grant degrees to women.

community colleges, four French and five English. The Maritime Forest Ranger School in Fredericton and the School of Fisheries at Caraquet reflect the need for trained personnel in key industries. The Craft School in Fredericton is one of only two in Canada offering a formal study of crafts.

## Bilingualism

New Brunswick is Canada's only officially bilingual province. The Official Languages of New Brunswick Act of 1969 guaranteed New Brunswickers the right to receive government services in either English or French. More recently, provincial legislation and the Canadian Charter of Rights and Freedoms have recognized the *collective* rights of the French and English communities to their distinct educational and cultural institutions.

## Revenue

To raise money to pay for its many services, the provincial government levies taxes. About 60 percent of New Brunswick's revenues are raised through provincial taxes on individual and business income, and from sales and property taxes. The balance comes from money transferred from the federal government in the form of "equalization payments," which are meant to maintain a national standard for services such as health care in all the provinces. Other expenses, like the construction of bridges, highways, schools and hospitals, are financed by both levels of government through borrowing.

## Politics

New Brunswick's two major political parties are the Liberals and the Progressive Conservatives. Since Confederation, New Brunswickers have tended to keep the same party in power for lengthy periods. The Conservatives governed under five different premiers from 1870 to 1883, followed by Liberal governments from 1883 to 1907 under six different premiers. Conservative Richard Hatfield broke all records, serving as premier for 17 years, from 1970 until 1987. But when New Brunswickers decided they had had enough, they did it with a vengeance, sending Liberals to all 58 seats in the legislature! Third parties have not done well in New Brunswick, although the United Farmers won 11 seats in the 1920 election. The Confederation of Regions Party, which opposes official bilingualism, won 8 seats to become the official opposition in the 1991 election. Occasionally, the New Democratic Party wins a seat as well.

CHAPTER 8

# The Economy

**E**ver since New Brunswick's sprawling river system provided easy access to its forests for the shipbuilding industry, transportation has been pivotal to the provincial economy. Distant from larger centres yet heavily dependent on exports from forests, mines, potato fields and local industries, New Brunswick has consistently turned to the federal government for policies favouring fast, cheap transportation, from the Intercolonial Railway in the 1870s to the Maritime Freight Rates Act in 1927.

Today, trucks are carrying the goods that used to travel by rail, with deteriorating road surfaces the result. The province has entered into a cost-sharing agreement with the federal government to expand the National Highway System from two lanes to four from the Quebec border to Nova Scotia and Cape Tormentine, and from the port of Saint John along the coast to the Maine border. In October 1993, the federal government and the governments of New Brunswick and Prince Edward Island signed an agreement with a contractor to build the long-awaited 13.3-kilometre (8.3-mile) bridge from Cape Tormentine to Borden, Prince Edward Island. Both provinces hope for economic benefits from the project.

Although their use is down, railways still serve the province. Canadian National operates two main freight lines, from the Nova Scotia border through Moncton, Grand Falls and Edmundston to Montreal, and up the northeast coast via Newcastle and Campbellton to Montreal. Despite considerable resistance from politicians, Canadian Pacific Rail has received federal permission to abandon its freight line from Saint John to Sherbrooke, Quebec.

**The rolling farmland of Victoria County in northwestern New Brunswick**

There is also daily passenger service on VIA Rail from Halifax to Moncton and on to Montreal by way of the northeastern and Saint John routes.

Resource industries like mining and forestry rely on the province's ports. Saint John handles the heaviest volume, largely refined oil and forest products. Dalhousie handles newsprint, mine concentrates and coal, and Belledune on the Bay of Chaleur moves ore concentrates, coal and fertilizer. Chatham-Newcastle is used by Miramichi paper mills, and as many as 150 other small ports serve small craft along the coasts and the Saint John River system.

The burgeoning information-based sector of the New Brunswick economy may explain the recent improvement in air transportation. Despite the province's relatively small population, seven airports now provide daily commercial air service. Fredericton, Moncton and Saint John offer daily flights to Toronto, Montreal and Boston.

*Right:* The setting sun casts a warm glow over the Trans-Canada Highway and the Saint John River. *Far right:* The port of Saint John offers excellent year-round facilities for ocean-going vessels and container shipping.

## Forestry

In 1832, John McGregor visited a New Brunswick logging camp and wrote:

> No course of life can undermine the constitution more than that of a lumberer and raftsman. The winter, snow and frost, although severe, are nothing to endure in comparison to the extreme coldness of the snow-water of the freshets, in which the lumberer is, day after day, wet up to the middle.

Things have changed a lot since the 1830s. Logging has become increasingly mechanized, and men no longer have to stand, day after day, in icy streams. But the province's forests continue to play an enormous role in the provincial economy.

Today, one out of every eight New Brunswick workers depends directly or indirectly on the forest for a living. A quarter of all goods produced in New Brunswick, including about half of the exports, is related to forestry. Pulp mills have helped to urbanize

**Forestry and its related industries have always played an important role in the province's economy. Seen here: (*left*) pulp and paper mill at Saint John; (*below*) logging operation at Nash Creek, near the Bay of Chaleur shore**

the province, drawing workers off the farm to the towns and cities.

The paper you are looking at right now was made from *wood pulp,* a mixture of water, cellulose fibres from wood, and a wood extract called *lignin* to bind the fibres. Of the $1.3 billion produced each year by New Brunswick forests, about three-quarters comes from the pulp and paper industry, which employs two-thirds of the 14 000 people working in forestry. Some mills produce finished products, while others export the pulp or the pulpwood.

New Brunswick wood lots also yield close to a million Christmas trees, 90 percent of which are sold in the United States. Other forest products include maple syrup, shingle bolts, and hardwood and softwood sawlogs and studwood. But trees don't have to be cut or tapped to prove their economic value. New Brunswickers and tourists alike are drawn to the province's glorious woodlands for hiking, canoeing, fishing and hunting. The display of colours in areas like Mount Carleton Provincial Park in the north and Sussex in the south attracts busloads of tourists every fall. Without a doubt, New Brunswick's 6 million hectares (15 million acres) of productive forest land are a resource worth preserving.

Some of the logging industry's practices are controversial — especially clear-cut harvesting,which the big forest companies prefer for its efficiency. Some people have objected to the chemical pesticides used to control the spruce budworm, a moth whose larvae attack spruce and fir needles and which wiped out whole forests in the 1920s. They cite possible damage to human and animal health and the disruption of the forest's natural life cycle.

Both the federal and provincial governments support the forest industry through research, education and financial assistance for experimental practices. The province operates three nurseries that raise mainly black spruce and jack pine seedlings to reforest Crown lands and private woodlots.The Maritime Forest Ranger School in Fredericton, the Faculty of Forestry at the University of

New Brunswick and the École des sciences forestières in Edmundston offer degrees in forestry.

## Fisheries and Aquaculture

Well before there was a New Brunswick, people were fishing here. The Micmacs and Maliseets set weirs, speared salmon, and smoked fish for winter. Today's fishery ranks fourth in output among the province's primary industries. The three major fishing regions are the Bay of Fundy, the Northumberland Strait and the Gulf of St. Lawrence. The industry includes fishing, fish processing (freezing, canning, salting and smoking) and aquaculture, or fish farming.

Fishing employs about 8000 people, who annually land 150 000

*Top left and below:* **The net weirs that are used to catch young herring along the Bay of Fundy coasts look much like those the Micmac used to make with wood brush hundreds of years ago. The fish feeding near the surface at high tide are trapped in the corral-like weir when the tide recedes. They are then easily scooped up in large nets called** *seines. Below left:* **Getting ready to set out the crab traps at Cap-Pelé on the Northumberland Strait**

tonnes of fish and shellfish, including farmed salmon. The New Brunswick fleet has three divisions: the *offshore* fishery, which includes shrimp trawlers, herring boats and the groundfish (cod, haddock, flounder) fleet; the *midshore,* which includes a large crab fleet; and the *inshore,* which fishes lobster, herring, mackerel, groundfish and scallops. The catch varies considerably from year to year, but the crustaceans, especially snow crab, shrimp and lobster, tend to be the most valuable. Herring is abundant, but the price is not high.

With the decline of the Atlantic salmon due to overfishing and habitat degradation, the government has been encouraging aquaculture. In fact, the Department of Fisheries is now the Department of Fisheries and Aquaculture. To date, fish farmers raise salmon and rainbow trout, but mussel and oyster culture are growing enterprises. The number of sites where salmon are raised has soared from one in 1979 to 64 in 1993, and production has increased a thousandfold. With its eye on increased world competition, the government is encouraging experiments with other species, including arctic char, striped bass, halibut, haddock and winter flounder.

About 13 000 New Brunswickers are employed canning, freezing, salting or smoking fish in about 150 processing plants, large and small. They marinate herring and freeze snow crab and lobster, and small smokehouses have reintroduced the traditional art of fish smoking to supply a growing appetite for fine smoked salmon. These plants don't just process the fish caught in New Brunswick waters; the tuna processed in the Star-Kist plant in St. Andrews is imported, as are the sardines processed at Connors Bros. in Blacks Harbour, one of only two sardine processors in Canada. The total value of processed fish, which is exported to over 50 countries, was $340 million in 1988.

Conservation of fish stocks is not a new concern in New Brunswick. Back in 1850, Captain John Robb of the sloop *Satellite* complained that Grand Manan fishermen caught so many tons of unwanted baby herring in their weirs that they used them for fertilizer; he was afraid that the fish waste they dumped on shore would contaminate the commercial fisheries. Because the modern New Brunswick fishery does not rely heavily on groundfish, it has been spared the massive unemployment caused in other parts of Atlantic Canada by the depletion of cod stocks and the closure of that fishery. Currently, however, there are concerns about several stocks; commercial salmon fishing is banned, and all other species, especially the crab and lobster stocks, are regularly monitored.

## Agriculture

Despite the richness of the soil along the Saint John River valley, it has never been easy to make a living from farming. In the 1920s, many farmers had to rely on part-time work in logging, fishing or construction to make ends meet, and the exodus from farms began. In 1931, 44 percent of New Brunswickers lived on farms. By 1961, the figure was 11 percent, and by 1991, it was down to 1.5 percent.

*Left:* **Although the dairy industry is concentrated mainly in the south, occasional dairy farms can be found in most areas of the province. This one, located near New Mills, enjoys a wonderful view of the Bay of Chaleur.** *Right:* **Potato field in bloom near Grand Falls.** *Inset:* **Bagging seed potatoes at Saint-Quentin**

Together, the income from potato and dairy production accounts for 43 percent of New Brunswick's farm income. The most important crop, potatoes, amounts to 20 percent of Canada's total production. A variety of types is planted, including seed potatoes for export to the United States. The potato-processing industry is centred at three plants in the rich upper Saint John River valley. At McCain Foods' two experimental farms near Florenceville, scientists have researched potato varieties from around the world. The dairy industry is concentrated in the south. The province is self-sufficient in milk, and also has a dairy-processing industry. To feed their cows, farmers produce grain and forage.

In addition to seed and table potatoes, New Brunswick exports blueberries and other small fruit, vegetables, livestock and processed foods throughout North America and around the world.

New Brunswick's 3200 farms directly employ about 5000 people, but the activity they generate in processing, transportation and service industries accounts for over 10 000 additional jobs.

## Mining and Energy

When Abraham Gesner, New Brunswick's first provincial geologist, explored the province from 1838 to 1842, he discovered a wide range of rocks and minerals and reported that coal fields underlay one-third of the province. When miners took him at his word and rushed to stake claims, they discovered he was wrong about the amount of coal — and Gesner was fired!

About one thing Gesner was right: this is a mineral-rich province, although it was not until the discovery of a major lead-zinc deposit near Bathurst in 1952 that mining became an important industry. As of 1992, New Brunswick ranked first in Canada in production of bismuth and zinc, second in lead, peat and silver, third in sulphur, and fourth in cadmium. New Brunswick is the only Canadian producer of marl, a type of clay used as fertilizer.

Base metals (zinc, lead, copper and silver) extracted at two mines

**Mines at Bathurst in northeastern New Brunswick. The area has about 40 percent of Canada's reserves of silver, lead and zinc.**

near the Bathurst-Newcastle area make up 64 percent of all minerals produced. Just southwest of Fredericton, near Lake George, is one of the oldest mines in the province, rumoured to be haunted by the ghost of miner Sam Hoskins, who died there in the late 1800s. Once Canada's only source of antimony, a product used in flameproofing children's clothing, the mine was recently closed.

Non-metallic resources such as peat and potash are next in importance. Trains from the rich potash mines in Sussex carry this fertilizer component to Saint John, where it is shipped to Latin America, Europe, Africa and Asia.

If you have ever started seeds in little Jiffy pots, you have used peat moss produced in Shippagan. The producers, located primarily in the northeast along the Acadian peninsula, range from small family operations to major international companies.

Although it did not underlie one-third of New Brunswick, coal was an important fuel in the 1800s, when the province was dotted with coal mines. Today, the province's only coal mine, located at Minto, fuels the New Brunswick Electric Power Commission's generators in Dalhousie and Grand Lake.

South of Moncton is the Stoney Creek oil field, operated by Irving Oil and a subsidiary. But New Brunswick is not dependent exclusively on fossil fuels. Alternative energy sources include the hydro-electric dams at Mactaquac (near Fredericton), Beechwood and Grand Falls and the nuclear power station at Point Lepreau. Proposals for a second nuclear reactor at Point Lepreau remain controversial because of the danger of nuclear accidents and the problem of nuclear waste disposal.

## Industry

Manufacturing and construction account for 20 percent of New Brunswick jobs. Forest products make up almost a third of manufacturing, followed by food and beverage processing, especially frozen potatoes and fish. Chemical products and the processing of mined resources are also significant. Two major construction projects, the Trans-Canada Highway expansion from the Nova Scotia border to Quebec and the Fixed Link to Prince Edward Island, are expected to generate thousands of temporary jobs in the 1990s.

## Two Enterprising Families

The New Brunswick economy would be vastly different without two local families — the McCains of Florenceville and the Irvings of Bouctouche. So dependent is the province on their enterprises that its economy has been described as the Irvings, the McCains and "the shrimps."

Kenneth Colin Irving, who died at the age of 93 in 1992, built an enormous and highly diversified business empire from the ground up. He began by selling Model T Fords and gasoline in his home town. When Imperial Oil cancelled his contract in 1923, he got a $2000 bank loan, bought a dilapidated storage tank and went into business for himself. By the time of his death, his family owned about 300 companies in Atlantic Canada and New England. The total worth of the Irving conglomerate is estimated at $6 billion. The Irving oil refinery in Saint John is the largest in Canada; Irving's Saint John Shipbuilding landed a $3 billion contract to build the navy's 12 patrol frigates in 1983; Irving Pulp and Paper

*Far left:* **The Irving oil refinery at Saint John.** *Above:* **Fertilizer plant at Belledune.** *Left:* **Sardine processing. Some 13 000 New Brunswickers are employed in about 150 fish processing plants.**

has three mills near Saint John. The Irving family owns a fleet of ships larger than the Canadian Navy's, several trucking lines, a bus line, thousands of gas stations and convenience stores, all the English daily newspapers in New Brunswick, radio and television stations, and many other enterprises. One in 12 New Brunswickers is employed by an Irving enterprise.

Under K. C. Irving's business philosophy of "vertical integration," a network of Irving-owned companies supply one another, eliminating competition. Irving oil shipped by Irving-built tankers is delivered in Irving trucks to Irving plants guarded by Irving security guards.

Inevitably, an individual of K. C. Irving's wealth and power was controversial. His support for any provincial government tended to last only so long as government legislation did not interfere with Irving interests. So Premier Louis Robichaud demonstrated considerable courage when he took on Irving three times. He allowed a competitor, Rothesay Paper, to set up shop in the province, reduced the Irving interest in Brunswick Mining to minority status and persisted with his Program of Equal Opportunity over Irving's strong objections to its tax provisions. Irving never forgave Robichaud, and moved in late 1971 to Bermuda. When he died, the Moncton *Times-Transcript* commented, "It is pointless to try to imagine what New Brunswick would be like had K. C. Irving not been such a success. It would be a drastically different place and undoubtedly worse off."

Behind New Brunswick's second most important industry, food processing, is the McCain family. The original business, McCain Produce, started to export seed potatoes from Florenceville in 1914. McCain Foods began producing frozen French fries there in 1957. Today, McCain has facilities in Florenceville and Grand Falls, in Prince Edward Island, Ontario, Quebec, Manitoba and Alberta. It is a major international food processor, with more than 45 facilities in nine countries on three continents. You can buy the company's French fries in London, Paris, New York, Sydney and Tel Aviv. McCain has diversified into equipment and transportation. Its subsidiary Day and Ross runs a fleet of more than 500 refrigerated trailers.

## Industrial Decline, Service Industry Revival

Industrial decline has been a harsh reality in New Brunswick since the end of the Golden Age of Sail in the 1880s. In the 1980s, manufacturing in firms with more than 100 employees declined by about 30 percent, and unemployment remained high. Small businesses, however, generated new jobs, especially in the communications field.

Fully 70 percent of the jobs in New Brunswick are in the service sector — transportation, communications, finance, insurance, real estate, education, medicine, trade, government and tourism. Moncton, with its bilingual work force, has recently experienced a boom in the telecommunications field. Datacor/ISM, Atlantic Canada's most advanced information systems management centre, chose Moncton as home base, as did Lexitech, a company breaking new ground in fully automated machine translation. Attracted by new communications systems developed by New Brunswick's innovative telephone company, NBTel, Purolator Courier recently moved its supercentre to Moncton, as have other national couriers.

## Tourism

Tourism contributed $575 million to the New Brunswick economy in 1991, employing 21 600 people. As the gateway to the Maritime provinces, New Brunswick is well-placed to attract tourists. Other attractions are the diversity of its natural settings, the province's rich history and its bilingual culture.

**A small sampling of the charms that bring tourists by the thousands to New Brunswick every year: (*left*) orchard near Oromocto in the spring; (*right*) East Quoddy Lighthouse, Campobello Island**

# CHAPTER 9

# Arts and Recreation

New Brunswick's artists seem to thrive on the province's geographical isolation. Although they have kept in touch with current trends, their very remoteness from metropolitan centres has allowed them to clarify their independent visions and styles.

## Visual Arts

The first Canadian university to award a Bachelor of Fine Arts degree (in 1941) was Mount Allison, in the small town of Sackville. For close to a century, the fine arts had been taught there (at the Female Academy, later the Ladies' College), by a highly skilled and largely female faculty. From 1916 to 1935 Elizabeth McLeod, an accomplished still-life painter, administered the art department. Christian Harris McKiel, a fine portraitist, headed the new Department of Applied Arts in 1938.

Toronto-born Lawren P. Harris, son of a member of the Group of Seven, directed the program from 1946 to 1975, executing some highly abstract, geometric paintings as well as realistic portraits and murals and mosaics for the university campus. The influential "magic realist" painter Alex Colville taught at Mount Allison from 1946 to 1963. Even today student art work occasionally reflects Colville's meticulous, hauntingly realistic style.

Montreal-born David Silverberg replaced Colville in 1963. The exceptional quality of line, colour and technique in his engravings of the mothers and children, flowers and animals he sketches in Europe, Asia and South America has attracted international recognition.

*The Beach* by Molly Lamb Bobak

*Right:* This dramatic sculpture at Escuminac is Claude Roussel's memorial to 35 local fishermen who were lost at sea in 1959. *Far right:* In addition to landscapes, Jack Humphrey produced many fine portraits, including this one, entitled *Jean,* of his wife. *Below:* Ned Bear's powerful masks testify to the enduring strength of Native traditions.

Saint John has nurtured several important twentieth-century artists. The powerful human figures of painter Miller Brittain demonstrate three distinct styles. His sympathetic realist paintings of the working-class people of Saint John contrast strongly with both his semi-surrealist paintings of heads or bodies in strangely eerie landscapes and his highly charged religious works. Although Jack Humphrey returned from a visit to France in 1954 to develop abstract techniques, he is probably best known for his earlier, more traditional portaits and watercolour landscapes of woods and shore.

Two important Fredericton artists are the Bobaks — Bruno, the Polish-born expressionist painter, and Molly Lamb, who has illustrated the popular children's poetry books of Fredericton writer-performer Sheree Fitch.

The Galerie d'Art de l'Université de Moncton was founded in 1965 under the directorship of sculptor Claude Roussel. The university

There is little doubt that the most impressive painting in the Beaverbrook Gallery is the huge *Santiago el Grande* by Spanish surrealist Salvador Dali, bought for the gallery's opening in 1959.

and its gallery have been pivotal in the flourishing of the arts in the Acadian community. Roussel's sculptures use a variety of media — bronze, metal rods, precast concrete, stone and wood. Another important Acadian artist is Herménégilde Chiasson, known for his highly personal prints and drawings, as well as his films, plays and poetry. Yvon Gallant's work observes the daily scene in Moncton, while Nancy Morin uses vivid oils to give romantic renderings of snakes and the moon. Marie-Hélene Allain's enormous stone sculptures can be seen throughout the province; one stands outside the Beaverbrook Gallery in Fredericton.

That gallery, with its important collection of major Canadian and international works, has enhanced the city's reputation. Its Canadian holdings include the world's largest public collection of Cornelius Krieghoffs, works by most of the Group of Seven artists and paintings by Brittain, Humphrey and Colville.

Micmac and Maliseet artists look to their roots for traditional techniques and spiritual inspiration. Paintings by Shirley Bear of Tobique Reserve integrate the patterns of ancient Micmac petroglyphs (rock drawings) with her own richly coloured figurative style. The wood and clay work of sculptor Luke Simon of Big Cove demonstrates his knowledge of many aboriginal cultures. Ned Bear produces severe, unsmiling masks that reflect his concern for the future of his culture. By teaching young people to carve, he hopes to transmit and preserve this heritage.

## Crafts

The history of craft production in New Brunswick begins with the Native peoples, whose intricate porcupine-quill weaving impresses modern collectors just as it did the early Europeans. Today, New Brunswick's reputation for fine crafts extends as far as Europe and Japan. The New Brunswick Crafts School in Fredericton is one of only two schools in Canada devoted exclusively to crafts.

The first settlers' crafts often grew from necessity. Wool and flax were spun and woven at home, and rug-hooking was a popular art. In the New Brunswick Museum you can see a rug hooked entirely from corn husks in 1841 by Mary Ann Toole of King's County. Acadian women were noted for their fine gold thread embroidery on church vestments.

New Brunswick's native woods, including bird's eye maple, butternut and linden, have attracted fine woodcarvers and sculptors, like Moncton's Claude Roussel and Bathurst's Gilbert LeBlanc.

The province's landscapes also influence design. Charlotte Glencross's three-dimensional tapestry "Never the same . . . twice" was inspired by canoeing on the Miramichi, and Tom Smith has done a pottery series entitled "Landscapes of the Fundy Coast."

**Foremost among New Brunswick's craftspeople are Native beadworkers and the internationally renowned Madawaska weavers.**

## Theatre

In New Brunswick, theatre is a lively art. Theatre troupes do not limit themselves to the standard repertoire of Broadway, Paris, Molière and Shakespeare. In both official languages, they perform plays written by New Brunswickers, often about local themes.

The Playhouse in Fredericton is home to Theatre New Brunswick, founded in 1968. Although based in the capital, this company regularly braves icy roads and storms to tour eight centres and 90 schools annually.

TNB has not laboured alone in encouraging the development of a local theatre tradition. Fredericton's Calithumpians perform comedy in their peculiar French-English patois in Officers' Square. Sackville's summer company, Live Bait, frequently features plays by New Brunswick comedy writer Norm Foster. Professional theatre has been attracted to Moncton with the restoration of its vintage 1922 Capitol Theatre. In November 1993, Tchaikovsky's

*Left:* **Caraquet's Théâtre Populaire d'Acadie in a production of Laurier Melanson's** *Zélika à Cochon Vert. Right:* **A Theatre New Brunswick production of** *Wrong for Each Other* **by New Brunswick playwright Norm Foster.**

ballet *The Nutcracker* was mounted there by DancEast, a young, semi-professional company that has successfully toured Europe.

Since 1974, Caraquet's Théâtre Populaire d'Acadie has produced plays by Régis Brun, Laval Goupil and Antonine Maillet, among other Acadian playwrights. Moncton's French company, Théâtre l'Escaouette, founded in 1978, originally toured the province's schools. Almost half its repertoire is by Herménégilde Chiasson.

## Music

Every year in early August, Newcastle erupts into song, fiddle music and step dancing during the Miramichi Folk Song Festival, which celebrates both local and international folk music. The festival was founded in 1958 by New Brunswick folklorist Louise Manny to preserve the local folk tradition and encourage new songs.

New Brunswick folksongs have long roots, reaching back to France, England, Scotland and Ireland. When a group of Moncton students sang the Acadian sea song "Partons, la mer est belle" on a wharf in France one summer, a group of French sailors responded with their own version of it. English folk music includes lumberjack songs like "Bruce's Log Camp" and sea shanties like "The Sailor's Lament." The popular bilingual Quigley Ensemble takes a unique folk/jazz approach to songs from many traditions, including Acadian, Scottish, Hebrew, and Black blues music.

Acadian classical choral music draws on this folk tradition, as well as on the hymns and Gregorian chants of the Catholic Church. New Brunswick's choirs have received frequent international attention. Between 1950 and 1965, the Notre Dame d'Acadie choir won the Lincoln Trophy for the best amateur choir of Canada five times. The Jeunes Chanteurs d'Acadie, founded in 1966 by Sister Lorette Gallant, won three first prizes at the 1974 International Music Eisteddfod in Wales. The Hillsborough Girls' Choir from Moncton won third prize there and first at the Vienna International Festival in 1988.

Two New
Brunswickers who
have become stars
well beyond their
own borders: Roch
Voisine and Edith
Butler

One of New Brunswick's oldest Acadian and English musical traditions is fiddling. The English New Brunswick fiddle style, with its distinct, unslurred notes, was developed and popularized by New Brunswick–born Don Messer, whose radio and television shows were favourites with audiences across the country for over 40 years. Riverview's Ivan Hicks is a two-time winner of the Maritime Fiddling Championship and was inducted into the North American Fiddlers' Hall of Fame.

Of course, New Brunswick has its rock musicians, too — most notably, Roch Voisine. Born in Saint-Basile in 1963, Voisine started composing music at 14. "Hélène," the title song of his first album, caused a sensation in Paris in 1990 and his hit "I'll Always Be There" helped him win the Juno Award for male vocalist of 1993.

## Acadian Writers

One Acadian writer, Antonine Maillet of Bouctouche, can be credited with the recent blossoming of Acadian literature. In 1972 she published *La Sagouine* , the fictional reminiscences of a 72-year-old charwoman. Delivering her salty monologues in a rich local dialect, Maillet's Sagouine muses philosophically and often hilariously on a variety of themes — the government, war, life and

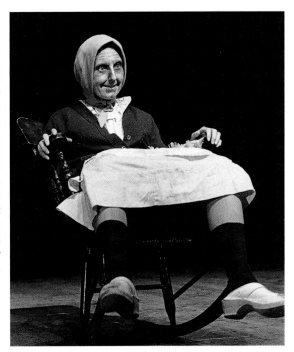

Viola Léger as Antonine Maillet's *La Sagouine*. The Acadian actress's rendition of the wry comments Maillet put into her best-known character's mouth ("It's been 200 years, 'n we're still alive. We go on ploughin' those weed fields of ours, 'n fishin' fer clams, oysters 'n smelts. We still try to make ends meet 'n not to die before passin' away.") helped make the staged version of the novel a major hit across the country.

death. A later novel, *Pélagie-la-Charrette* , won the esteemed French literary prize, the Prix Goncourt, in 1979. Maillet was the first non-French author ever accorded this honour.

Meanwhile, others were collecting Acadian folk material. Father Anselme Chiasson collected the popular traditions of Nova Scotia's Chéticamp community and other regions, Melvin Gallant published eight folktales with the comical character Ti-Jean (a close relation of the "Jack" in "Jack and the Beanstalk"), and Louis Haché wrote about the island of Miscou and the Acadian peninsula.

The first Acadian publishing house, Les Éditions d'Acadie, entered the scene in 1973 with Raymond LeBlanc's *Cri de terre*. LeBlanc was one of many angry young poets in the 1970s who warned that French was drowning in the surrounding English sea. In his powerful *Mourir à Scoudouc* (1974) Herménégilde Chiasson approaches the same theme with pessimism, while Clarence Comeau, in *Entre amours et silences* (1980), speaks of Acadians as "children of a race/Which knocks/On Justice's door."

## English Writers

> Over time, living in such a small place, you come to see and share in the unfolding of many lives . . . The ranges of your perception open and grow like circles in a pool after the stone has disappeared.

Sackville author Ann Copeland's words aptly describe the attraction living in New Brunswick holds for many writers — an exposure to the lives of a wide spectrum of people. Alden Nowlan, whose poetry collection *Bread, wine and salt* won the Governor General's Award in 1967, focused sympathetically yet honestly on poor and downtrodden characters. The gifted novelist and Governor General's Award winner David Adams Richards gives voice to the Miramichi working class in novels like *Lives of Short Duration, Nights Below Station Street* and *For Those Who Hunt the Wounded Down*. In her own story collection *Earthen Vessels*, Ann Copeland writes of characters ranging from young widows to penitentiary inmates.

The New Brunswick landscape has inspired many writers, most notably lyric poet Bliss Carman, considered one of Canada's finest poets in his lifetime (1861-1929), and Sir Charles G. D. Roberts. Much of Roberts's writing is imbued with the history and landscape of the Tantramar River region, where he spent his boyhood exploring the tidal marshes and woods. Together with Ontario's Ernest Thompson Seton, he is credited with inventing the realistic animal story — the only literary genre created by Canadians.

## Sports

For the Micmacs and Maliseets who lived in New Brunswick before the Europeans arrived, sports offered a way to perfect the physical skills that their lives as hunters and travellers along the region's rivers and bays required. The Maliseet of the Saint John River valley used to gather at Ekw-pa-hakw (Savage Island) near Fredericton for foot and canoe races. Legend has it that in the early nineteenth century a stagecoach driver once refused a ride to a Maliseet named

New Brunswickers took enthusiastically to baseball, and by the turn of the century, there were Black baseball teams and women's teams. Seen here, the Saint John Royals displaying their trophies and the Bocabec, Charlotte County, girls' team

Peter Lola. So fast was Lola on foot, however, that the coach arrived in Woodstock to find him waiting!

In a province where baseball, curling, golf, skating, skiing, hiking, canoeing, wind-surfing and swimming are increasingly popular, sports form a part of most people's lives. But in earlier days, sports like cricket, football and curling were reserved for soldiers of the British garrison, who had plenty of spare time. In Saint John, men of the 72nd Highland regiment got a local stonemason to fashion curling stones, which they bequeathed to the townspeople for the city's first curling match, on New Year's Day, 1854.

By then, merchants and clerks had leisure hours for sports like curling, but labourers worked six long days a week and were expected to refrain from frivolity on the Sabbath. Still, fishermen and lumber raftsmen often held impromptu boat races on the job.

Skating was one of the first mass-participation sports. In 1863, a writer from New York wrote glowingly about Saint John's Victoria Rink, and by 1886, the J. A. Whelpley Skate Company was producing 12 000 skates annually. Baseball was introduced to Saint John in 1869 by P. A. Melville, a prominent newspaperman.

Women in New Brunswick found a place on the sports scene early. The Saint John Golf Club had 60 female members in 1900. Mabel

Summer and winter, New Brunswickers take advantage of the many opportunities the province provides them to participate in sports.

Thompson won the national Open Amateur Championship for women in 1902 and again from 1905 to 1908.

The New Brunswick Sports Hall of Fame, established in 1970, recognizes a wide range of the province's top athletes. Charlie Gorman, having decided to forego a career in baseball for speedskating, proceeded to win the American, Canadian and North American championships. Then, in 1926, he won the World Speedskating Championship at Lily Lake in Saint John. Yvon "Fighting Fisherman" Durelle, of Baie Sainte-Anne, won Canadian and British Empire Light-Heavyweight Championships in the 1950s. Willie Eldon O'Ree of Fredericton, the first Black hockey player in the National Hockey League, played with the Boston Bruins in 1958 and in 1960-61. Ron Turcotte of Drummond rode the great horse Secretariat to win racing's Triple Crown in 1973, a feat that had not been achieved for 25 years. He was also the first jockey to win back-to-back Kentucky Derbies since 1902. Sandra Lea DeVenney, a founding member of the New Brunswick Wheelchair Association, won 56 medals between 1971 and 1978 at the Canadian Wheelchair Games. And New Brunswick finally achieved a stake in major league baseball when local hero Rhéal Cormier of Saint-André began pitching for the St. Louis Cardinals in 1991.

# CHAPTER 10

# Around New Brunswick

The history of New Brunswick was shaped by the rivers that traverse its rich forests and the sea that attracted fishermen and shipbuilders. Let us follow both around the province, beginning our tour where the Loyalists first glimpsed their new home, at the mouth of the Saint John River.

## The Saint John River Valley

Winding almost 700 kilometres (435 miles) through a hilly valley of broad green vistas and lush forests, from northern Maine to the Bay of Fundy, the Saint John has been called the "Rhine of North America." At Saint John, the river meets the tidal waters of the Bay of Fundy. Twice a day, the powerful tidal flow forces the river water back up a narrow gorge creating the phenomenon known as the Reversing Falls.

A visitor's first impression of Saint John itself may be coloured by the city's industrial aspects. This quickly changes, however, with the discovery of Saint John's charming restorations.

In the renovated Barbour's General Store, where the brothers George and William set up shop in 1867, visitors can see what shopping was like a century ago. Those who pass through the wrought-iron gates of the old City Market, which was opened in 1876, can still buy fruits, vegetables, meats, cheeses and dulse — the toasted reddish seaweed that New Brunswickers eat as a snack.

Saint John today (*clockwise from centre*): Town crier; Market Square, part of an extensive waterfront renovation that has helped revive the downtown core; detail of the restored plasterwork in the Imperial Theatre built in 1913; old City Market; Saint John Harbour; performers from all across Canada come to the Festival By The Sea

The New Brunswick Museum, Canada's oldest, introduces the visitor to the province's natural and human history. That history comes alive at the Carleton Martello Tower, constructed at the port of Saint John between 1813 and 1815 to fend off an American invasion during the War of 1812. An impressive, thick-walled structure, the tower stood idle until 1866, when it became a watchpost against a threatened invasion by the Fenians. During World War II it was a co-ordination centre for coastal defences.

Heading northwest towards Fredericton, travellers may criss-cross the tranquil valleys of the Saint John, Belleisle and Kennebecasis rivers several times on underwater-cable ferries invented in 1904 by Captain William Abraham Pitt. Approaching Oromocto, the land flattens. Spring floods make it more fertile, yielding bumper crops of vegetables and abundant apple orchards — a blur of pink in the spring, blazing scarlet in the fall.

The visitor gets a foretaste of Fredericton's gentility driving along the willow-lined banks of the river, which mirrors the spire of

**Fredericton (***clockwise from near right***):** Officers' Square with a statue of Lord Beaverbrook; Christ Church Cathedral, one of the finest examples of decorated Gothic architecture in North America; University of New Brunswick nestled in the hills overlooking the Saint John River; stately old homes reflect an earlier era

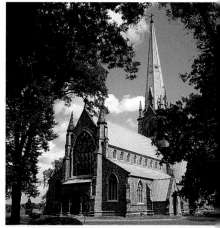

Christ Church Cathedral, the legislature dome and the campus of the University of New Brunswick. Many of the elegant frame houses built along the capital's elm-lined streets date from the eighteenth or early nineteenth century. The Beaverbrook Art Gallery and the Playhouse Theatre were gifts from native New Brunswicker Lord Beaverbrook. At Boyce Market, Fredericton's small immigrant communities add a wide range of foods — Lebanese stuffed grapevine leaves, spicy Indian samosas, Vietnamese spring rolls — to local specialties such as fiddleheads and rhubarb.

West of Fredericton the Saint John River forms a vast headpond above the Mactaquac Hydro Dam, the largest operating hydroelectric generating station in the Maritimes. On the south shore of the river at Kings Landing Historical Settlement, the traveller suddenly slips back in time. In a cluster of homes dating from the early to the late 1800s, costumed residents live the daily life of New Brunswick Loyalists, drying herbs for cooking and medicinal use, carding and spinning wool. Each summer, New Brunswick children become "Visiting Cousins" for a week. They carry water, make soap and butter, and attend the tiny, one-room school where they sing "The King" and do sums on slates.

North of Nackawic, a pulp and paper mill town, the river narrows as it continues towards Hartland and the world's longest covered bridge. Florenceville is the home base of McCain Foods, one of the world's largest producers of processed and frozen foods. Further to the northwest is the bilingual community of Grand Falls/Grand-Sault, named for its waterfall. According to Maliseet legend, the maiden Malabeam led an army of 300 Iroquois warriors over the torrent in revenge for the murder of her father. Today, the falls power the Grand Falls generating station.

Near the Quebec border at Edmundston is the mythical Republic of Madawaska in the most bilingual part of New Brunswick, where many people switch effortlessly from French to English and back again. Legend has it that the province won Madawaska County by a roll of the dice between Governor Thomas Carleton of New

*Top right:* The world's longest covered bridge (391 metres/1282 feet), at Hartland, was built in 1899. *Below right:* Creaking oxcarts carry visitors through the tranquil landscape of yesteryear at Kings Landing. *Far right:* Grand Falls on the Saint John River, a 23-metre (75-foot) waterfall

Brunswick and his brother Sir Guy, Governor of British North America at Quebec. Today the Republic of Madawaska displays its own coat of arms and its own flag, an eagle with six stars.

## Restigouche Uplands and the Acadian Coast

In the interior region known as the Restigouche Uplands, French is heard more often than English. Here are New Brunswick's wildest landscapes — deep forests, spectacular autumn colours and the highest peak in the Maritimes, Mount Carleton. Along Mount Carleton Provincial Park's ten trails, hikers can explore mountains, forests, valleys, rivers and lakes. Trees range from a rare stand of pure red pine, regenerated from a forest fire in 1933, to sugar maple, yellow and white birch, beech, pin cherry, mountain and black ash, spruce, fir, poplar and elm. Mountain cranberries and blueberries are ripe for picking in September, and from the mountain peak the adventurous can catch a panoramic view of Mount Sagamook, Mount Bailey and the Nepisiguit Lakes.

Northeast on the Bay of Chaleur is the site of the Battle of the Restigouche. Here, in the spring of 1760, Lieutenant Charles des

*Left:* Mount Carleton, New Brunswick's highest peak (820 metres/2690 feet), is a hiker's delight with breathtaking scenery, moose sightings and fiddleheads in the spring. *Above:* Bathurst, at the mouth of the Nepisiguit River, is famous for its miles of sandy beaches, the warm waters of its bays and one of the finest golf courses in the Maritimes.

Champs de Boishébert and a force of Acadian privateers who had eluded deportation were defeated by the British, marking the final conquest of New France.

Near Dalhousie, just east of Campbellton, is the Eel River Sandbar, one of the longest natural sandbars in the world. On one side is fresh water, on the other the salt water of the Bay of Chaleur.

Driving along the bay on the north shore of the Acadian peninsula, the traveller reaches the Village Historique Acadien (Acadian Historical Village) at Caraquet. In hand-hewn wooden buildings, amidst *aboiteaux* duplicating early Acadian dykes, costumed staff recreate nineteenth-century Acadian life, carding, spinning and dying wool, churning butter, hammering a blacksmith's anvil and printing a newspaper. Just as some of the returned Acadian exiles found work in the fishing shed of Charles Robin, today's fishermen at the village's Robin Shed work on the hull of a new boat, repair nets and dry fish. And visitors are invited to help with the chores.

At the northeast tip of the peninsula is Shippagan, with its Aquarium and Marine Centre, and Canada's largest peat bogs. At nearby Lamèque, conductors, musicians and choirs come from around the world to perform at the annual International Festival of Baroque Music. A ferry ride away is Miscou Island, with long, unspoiled, sandy beaches and an 1856 lighthouse.

*Clockwise from top:* Miscou Island Ferry, one of New Brunswick's many underwater-cable ferries; Miscou Island with its wooden lighthouse, the oldest in operation in the Maritimes; Shediac hosts an annual world famous lobster festival with parades, folk songs and dancing, sports events and, of course, lobster dinners; Kelly's Beach, Kouchibouguac National Park

Moving south to the Gulf of St. Lawrence coast, the traveller passes Tracadie-Sheila, visited by Champlain in 1605.  Here Canada's first leper colony was established in 1868; its iron crosses remain in the old cemetery.  Further along the Gulf coast, south of Miramichi Bay, is one of New Brunswick's two national parks, Kouchibouguac, which reflects the variety of the region's landscapes — from sand dunes to peat bogs, tidal rivers to lagoons.

The Acadian village of Bouctouche is known as the birthplace of industrialist K. C. Irving and of Antonine Maillet, whose novel *La Sagouine* has captured the region's history and dialect.  Actors in the "Pays de la Sagouine" theme park bring to life Maillet's colourful characters — the charwoman of the title, her husband, Gapi, and La Sainte, her self-righteous neighbour.

The 200-metre (322-foot) suspension footbridge at McNamee. *Inset:* A lone fisherman casts for Atlantic salmon on the Miramichi River, famous as the best salmon river in the world.

## The Miramichi

Inland from coastal New Brunswick runs the province's most fabled river, the Miramichi, where royalty once went fishing for the king of gamefish, the silvery Atlantic salmon. Along the river system, outfitters rent out fishing equipment or take tourists out in their canoes. In the past the river was criss-crossed by swinging footbridges; only one remains, at McNamee.

The interior forest remains largely wilderness, where the screech of an eastern panther may occasionally be heard. This is logging country, dotted with pulpwood logs ready to be trucked to the mills in towns like Newcastle. Tourists can visit the Woodmen's Museum in Boiestown (the geographic centre of the province) to explore a logging camp kitchen and bunk house.

The original Irish settlers came to work in the woods and sawmills in the nineteenth century. Every July, the Miramichi Irish celebrate their heritage at their Irish Festival, which features traditional music and Irish games, foods and crafts. In August, during the Miramichi Folksong Festival, Newcastle resounds with traditional and contemporary music played by performers from the Miramichi, the rest of the province and well beyond.

101

The historic towns of Chatham and Newcastle. *Left to right:* Chatham hosts Canada's first and largest Irish festival each July; Newcastle's St. James and John United Church, built in 1829; The Miramichi Folk Festival brings dancers, musicians and history buffs to Newcastle every August.

## Fundy Coast

When Samuel de Champlain charted the Bay of Fundy in 1604, he must have been awed by the sheer variety of the coast, with its rugged cliffs, deep sandy beaches and grassy salt marshes.

On the St. Croix River, where the first Europeans spent the ill-fated winter of 1604-05, lies the border town of St. Stephen. Its cordial relationship with its American twin, Calais, goes back to the days of the War of 1812, when the two towns shared a Methodist minister named Duncan McColl. Preaching back and forth on both sides of the border, he established so much mutual trust that the St. Stephen garrison ran out of gunpowder during the war because they had lent it to the Americans to celebrate the Fourth of July! St. Stephen is home to Ganong Bros., Canada's oldest candy company, founded in 1873. Ganong made Canada's first lollipops using butchers' wooden skewers, produced the first chocolate bar in North America, and was the first company to sell Valentine candies in heart-shaped boxes.

For well over a century, tourists have come to the seaside resort of St. Andrews, with its red soil, delightful gardens and elegant architecture. Many famous people have kept summer homes here. Railway baron William Cornelius Van Horne built himself an

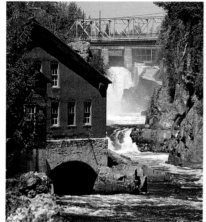

*Clockwise from top left:* The St. Croix River has the highest tides of any river in the world. Its many small rapids lure experienced and novice canoeists alike; St. Andrews, one of Canada's most beautiful seaside towns, is home to the Algonquin Resort Hotel, built in 1888; visitors appreciate walking tours of this historic village featuring stately homes, fine inns and stores, and craft shops and studios; Magaguadavic Falls, St. George. A fish ladder at the hydro dam above the falls assures the salmon can get upriver to spawn.

enormous mansion on nearby Ministers Island that can be reached from the mainland only at low tide. Covenhoven mansion has 12 bedrooms, 11 baths, 12 fireplaces and a solar greenhouse that provided the Van Hornes with fresh summer fruit year-round.

The islands of Passamaquoddy Bay are the traditional home of Passamaquoddy people, who still live on the American side of the Bay on lands reserved for them. Sometimes called the West Isles Archipelago, they include Campobello Island, the site of American president Franklin D. Roosevelt's beloved summer retreat. Boats take visitors through the bay for sightings of some 20 types of whales, and smaller marine mammals including dolphins, harbour porpoises and seals. The islands also attract arctic terns, blue herons, hawks, loons, ospreys and bald eagles. Rugged, tranquil Grand Manan Island, farther south in the bay, is even more of a paradise for birdwatchers: its Christmas bird count regularly totals more species than any other spot in the province.

Unspoiled beaches and red cliffs with caves to explore are found farther east in the tiny shipbuilding village of St. Martins, where 500 wooden ships were launched in the 1800s. Near the harbour are two covered bridges. According to tradition, courting couples would stop their buggies inside these "kissing bridges," which were built not to keep snow off the roads, but to protect the timbers from rotting. An open bridge might last 10 years, a covered one 80.

More covered bridges are found within the confines of Fundy National Park, which offers coastal cliffs, rolling, forested hills and breathtaking views of Chignecto Bay. Just northeast of Fundy, where the Petitcodiac River meets Shepody Bay, is Hopewell Cape. Over the millennia, glaciers, fractures and the incessant action of the Fundy tides have hollowed out caves and pillars in the rocky cliffs to form the peculiar, seaweed-draped "flowerpot rocks" that can be explored at low tide. At high tide, the rocks form small islands.

The Petitcodiac heads north to Moncton, a city that grew up in the 1870s with the railway. More recently, its bilingual workforce

*Right:* The 34-room Roosevelt Cottage is the focal point of Roosevelt-Campobello International Park on Campobello Island; *Below right:* Seal Cove, a picturesque fishing village on Grand Manan Island, the largest and most remote of the Fundy Isles. *Far right:* More than 250 species of birds have been sighted in the bird sanctuary on Grand Manan Island.

and knowledge-based resources have attracted national and international telecommunications companies. Southeast of Moncton is Dorchester, a quiet village of historic grey stone houses. Several have been restored to their nineteenth-century grandeur, including the Keillor House Museum.

On the Tantramar Marshes is the town of Sackville. Its boardwalked Waterfowl Park is haven for many species of birds that cross the Atlantic flyway. Here, tourists and residents alike watch and listen — for the hoarse cry of the American coot protecting its young, the rustle of a mallard's wings or the reappearance of a submerged pied-billed grebe. The town's three-day Atlantic Waterfowl Celebration won the Governor General's Award for Conservation in 1992. The boardwalk leads to the green, hilly campus of Mount Allison University, the first university in the British Empire to award a bachelor's degree to a woman.

*Above:* St. Martins, a shipbuilding capital in the days of sail, now is a fishing village and tourist centre.
*Top left:* The Moncton skyline seen from across the Petitcodiac River at low tide. *Middle left:* The annual Atlantic Hot Air Balloon Festival is held in Sussex every September.
*Below left:* Behind its rugged shoreline, Fundy National Park soars to a rolling plateau with stands of sugar maples, beech and yellow birch trees.

# Facts
## at a Glance

# General Information

**Entered Confederation:** July 1, 1867

**Origin of Name:** Named for the German duchy of Brunswick-Lunenburg of King George III

**Provincial Capital:** Fredericton

**Provincial Nickname:** Picture Province

**Provincial Flag:** A golden lion on a red compartment and an ancient oared galley

**Provincial Motto:** *Spem Reduxit* — "Hope was restored"

**Provincial Bird:** Black-capped chickadee

**Provincial Flower:** Purple violet

**Provincial Tree:** Balsam fir

**Languages:** New Brunswick is Canada's only officially bilingual province. About 64% of New Brunswickers are English-speaking, 33% French-speaking.

# Population

(1991 census)

**Population:** 723 900

**Population Density:** 9.8 persons per km²

**Population Distribution:** Urban 49%, rural 51%

**Cities:**

| | |
|---|---|
| Saint John | 74 969 |
| Moncton | 57 010 |
| Fredericton | 46 466 |
| Bathurst | 14 409 |
| Edmundston | 10 835 |
| Campbellton | 8 699 |

**Population Growth:**

| Year | Population |
|---|---|
| 1851 | 193 800 |
| 1871 | 285 594 |
| 1891 | 321 263 |
| 1911 | 351 889 |
| 1931 | 408 200 |
| 1941 | 457 400 |
| 1951 | 515 700 |
| 1961 | 597 900 |
| 1971 | 634 600 |
| 1981 | 696 400 |
| 1991 | 723 900 |

# Geography

**Borders:** New Brunswick is bordered on the north by Quebec and the Bay of Chaleur; on the west by the state of Maine; on the east by the Gulf of St. Lawrence and the Northumberland Strait; and on the south by the Bay of Fundy.

**Highest Point:** Mount Carleton, 820 m (2690 ft.)

**Lowest Point:** Sea level

**Area:** 73 437 km² ( 28 354 sq. mi.)

**Rank in area among provinces:**
Eighth

**Climate:** Coastal areas are warmer in winter and cooler in summer than inland areas. There is more precipitation in winter than in any other season, with the south coast getting the most. The annual snowfall averages about 244 cm (96 in.) a year. Coastal regions average -7°C (20°F) in January and 17°C (62°F) in July. Inland areas average -10°C (14°F) in January and 19°C (67°F) in July.

**National Parks:** Fundy National Park, Kouchibouguac National Park.

**Coasts:** New Brunswick has 2 269 km (1410 mi.) of jagged and varied coastline shaped by many bays and inlets. The Bay of Fundy is the largest bay and has the world's highest tides. Chaleur, Chignecto, Miramichi, and Passamaquoddy are the other major bays.

**Rivers and Waterfalls:** The Saint John River, the province's longest, flows 673 km (418 mi.). Beginning in Maine, it ranges through the western half of New Brunswick and the lower part of the Coastal Lowlands. Its branches are the Aroostook, Kennebecasis and Tobique rivers. The St. Croix River forms part of the New Brunswick–Maine border. Where the Bay of Chaleur narrows, the Restigouche River divides New Brunswick and Quebec. Other rivers include the Miramichi, Nepisiguit, and Petitcodiac.

The tides of the Bay of Fundy empty with great force into the Petitcodiac and other rivers in a high wave called a bore. At the mouth of the Saint John River, this produces the unique natural phenomenon of the Reversing Falls. In Grand Falls, the Saint John River dives 23 m (75 ft.).

**Lakes:** Grand Lake (181.3 km$^2$/70 sq. mi.), the largest lake in New Brunswick, forms an arm of the Saint John River. Other large lakes include Oromocto, Magaguadavic, Washademoak, and the Chiputneticook chain of lakes.

**Islands:** Campobello, Deer Island, Grand Manan, Miscou, Lamèque.

**Topography:** New Brunswick is divided into a few regions with distinct landscapes. The Central Highlands is a northern continuation of the Appalachian Mountain Range, formed about 380 million years ago. There are two other hilly regions, the Northern Uplands and the Southern Highlands, whose hills slope gently down to the Coastal Lowlands that border the sea.

# Nature

**Trees:** Pine, spruce, balsam fir, maple, ash, birch, cedar, ironwood, beech, elm, Eastern hemlock, tamarack, butternut, poplar, red oak.

**Wild Plants:** Purple violets and pink and white mayflowers are abundant in late spring. Berries include blackberries, blueberries, raspberries, and straw-berries. Fiddlehead ferns and other edible wild plants including goose tongues and samphire greens are plentiful.

**Land Mammals:** New Brunswick has 55 species of land mammals, including

**Red squirrel**

beaver, black bear, white-tailed deer, moose, lynx, coyote, red fox, porcupine, skunk and squirrel.

**Birds:** Almost 40% of all North American bird species have been sighted here. Shore birds include semipalmated sandpipers, the great blue heron and piping plover. Among waterfowl are the black duck, wood duck, green- and blue-winged teal and American coot. There are game birds such as partridge, pheasant and woodcock, and many other species, including the snowy owl, Atlantic puffin and black-capped chickadee.

**Fish and Shellfish:** Atlantic salmon, shad, brook trout, small-mouth bass, pickerel, cod, mackerel; lobster, mussels, clams, crabs.

**Sea Mammals:** Finback whale, minke whale, humpback whale, North Atlantic right whale, Atlantic white-sided dolphin, harbour porpoise.

## Connections and Communications

**By air:** Saint John, Fredericton and Moncton have major airports. All three are served by Air Canada and Air Nova. Air Atlantic also serves the province. Chatham, Bathurst, Charlo and a few smaller towns also have airports for commercial traffic.

**By sea:** Ferries travel to Nova Scotia and Prince Edward Island all year long and to Quebec in the summer. Saint John, Dalhousie and Caraquet have major commercial seaports.

**By road:** More than 4000 km (2485 mi.) of major highways run along the coastal areas and inland to Fredericton. The Trans-Canada Highway travels along the Saint John River, through Moncton, and from Aulac to Cape Tormentine.

**By rail:** Via Rail operates daily passenger service from Halifax to Montreal on two routes, one through Chatham, Bathurst and Campbellton, the other through Saint John, Fredericton and Maine. There are also three main freight lines.

**Newspapers:** Daily papers are Saint John's *Telegraph Journal* and *Evening Times Globe*, Fredericton's *The Gleaner*, and Moncton's *Times-Transcript*. *L'Acadie Nouvelle,* published in Caraquet, serves the francophone population daily. There are over 20 other weekly or monthly newspapers.

**TV and radio:** The province is served by three television networks, CBC, CTV and Radio-Canada. Many channels are available by satellite dish and cable. There are 53 French or English radio stations, including 10 French and 16 English CBC stations.

## Government and the Courts

**Federal:** New Brunswick has 10 seats in the House of Commons and 10 in the Senate.

**Provincial:** The Premier of New Brunswick, leader of the majority party in the legislature, heads the provincial government. The premier presides over the cabinet, the executive arm of the government. There are 58 members elected to the Legislative Assembly.

**The Courts:** New Brunswick's highest court, the Supreme Court, is made up of the Court of Queen's Bench and the Court of Appeals. The Court of Queens Bench has a trial and a family division. The Provincial Court handles criminal matters and Young Offenders cases.

**Local Government:** Run by mayors and elected councils, cities, towns and villages handle property matters such as fire protection and street, sewer and water service maintenance.

**Voting qualifications:** Voters in New Brunswick must be Canadian citizens of at least 18 years of age and residents of the province for at least six months.

## Education

**Universities:** New Brunswick's four universities are Mount Allison University (Sackville), Saint Thomas University (Fredericton), the Université de Moncton (Moncton, Edmundston and Shippagan), and the University of New Brunswick (Fredericton and Saint John). The province also has nine community college campuses, four of which serve the francophone community. Other educational institutions include the Maritime Forest Ranger School and the Craft School, in Fredericton, and the School of Fisheries at Caraquet.

New Brunswick has two parallel public school systems, one French and one English, with 450 schools from kindergarten to grade 12.

## Economy and Industry

**Mining and Energy:** Zinc, lead, silver, peat, potash, limestone, sand and gravel are the leading mining products. Hydro-electric and nuclear power are major energy industries, and some coal is produced locally.

**Agriculture:** New Brunswick's 3200 farms directly employ about 5000 people and generate 10 000 other jobs indirectly. Together, the income from potato and dairy production accounts for 43% of farm income. The most important crop is potatoes, 20% of Canada's total production. Self-sufficient in milk, New Brunswick has a dairy processing industry. Major food exports include seed and table potatoes, blueberries and other small fruit, vegetables, livestock and processed foods, primarily frozen potatoes.

**Fisheries:** Fishing employs about 8000 people, who landed 150 000 tonnes of fish and seafood, worth about $200 million in 1992. Major catches include lobster, shrimp, snow crab, herring, mackerel and scallops. Aquaculture, especially of salmon, is becoming increasingly profitable. More than 13 000 New Brunswickers are employed in about 150 fish processing plants.

**Tourism:** Tourism contributed $575 million to the economy in 1991 and employed 21 600 people.

**Forestry:** Trees of high economic value are red and black spruce for pulp and paper and balsam fir for Christmas trees. Aspen, beech, birch, cedar, maple, and pine also have economic value. About half of New Brunswick's forest is Crown Land. One out of eight New Brunswick workers depends either directly or indirectly on the forest for a living. Of the $1.3 billion produced each year by New Brunswick forests, about 75% is from the pulp and paper industry.

**Manufacturing:** Manufacturing and construction account for 20% of New Brunswick jobs, mostly processing primary products. Forest products — largely pulp, paper and plywood — account for about one-third of the net value of production, with food and beverage processing second in importance. Fully 70% of the jobs in New Brunswick are in the

"Visiting Cousins" at Kings Landing

service sector — transportation, communication and other utilities, finance, insurance, real estate, education and medicine, trade, government, and tourism.

## Social and Cultural Life

**Museums:** The province has 36 museums and art galleries. The Owens Art Gallery in Sackville, The Beaverbrook Gallery in Fredericton and the Galerie d'art at the Université de Moncton are the most prominent art galleries.

**Libraries:** The province has five regional public library systems with about 60 libraries. The largest is the Saint John Regional Library, with eight branches.

**Performing Arts:** The Saint John Symphony performs a broad repertoire. In July, musical theatre is presented by Rothesay's Kennebecasis Valley players. Theatre New Brunswick, based at the Playhouse in Fredericton, tours eight New Brunswick cities annually. In Sackville, the Live Bait Theatre Company performs at Mount Allison University during the summer. Two professional French-language theatres are Caraquet's Théâtre Populaire d'Acadie and Moncton's Théâtre l'Escaouette. Moncton is also New Brunswick's dance centre, with both DansEncorps and DancEast.

**Sports and Recreation:** Curling, golf, horseracing and boat races have long been popular among New Brunswickers. The province's long coastline and many rivers encourage water sports such as swimming, windsurfing, sailing and canoeing. Winter sports include skating, skiing, snowmobiling, hockey and ice-fishing.

## Historic Sites and Landmarks

*Acadian Historical Village,* in Caraquet, is a recreated settlement presenting the history and way of life of the Acadian people from 1780 to the early 1900s.

*Acadian Odyssey National Historic Site,* in Saint-Joseph de Memramcook, depicts Acadian history and culture through the work of Acadian artisans and through audio-visual displays.

*Fort Beauséjour National Historic Site,* in Aulac, dates from 1751. The visitor centre has paintings and artifacts reflecting local history. The restored ruins include underground areas and the earthworks of the historic fort.

*Fundy National Park* in Alma features camping, hiking, a golf course, and a heated salt-water

swimming pool with a panoramic view of the bay, cliffs and forested hills along the Fundy Coast.

*Kings Landing Historical Settlement* in Fredericton is a restored village from the Loyalist period (1784-1890), with more than 100 costumed staff living as New Brunswickers did over a century ago. It features a sawmill, gristmill, shops, farms and houses.

*Kouchibouguac National Park* on the Acadian coast is New Brunswick's largest park. Visitors can swim, camp, hike, bird-watch, canoe and cycle. The landscapes include beaches, sandbars, offshore dunes, tidal rivers, and warm lagoon waters.

*New Brunswick Legislative Assembly Building* in Fredericton contains a Portrait Gallery and an immense library. The main chamber can be

**New Brunswick Botanical Gardens, Atlantic Canada's only botanical gardens, at Saint-Jacques**

visited when the legislature is not in session.

*New Brunswick Museum* in Saint John, Canada's first museum, features various permanent exhibits illustrating New Brunswick's natural and human history. It houses frequent touring and temporary exhibits.

## Other Interesting Places

*Beaverbrook Art Gallery* in Fredericton features important works by Canadian and New Brunswick artists, as well as an impressive collection of 18th-century English art.

At *Grand Falls Gorge* in Grand Falls/Grand-Sault is New Brunswick's largest waterfall. The gorge encircles half the town.

*Hopewell Rocks* at Hopewell Cape are rocky cliffs sculptured by the Fundy tides. These seaweed-covered "flowerpot" rock formations can be explored at low tide. At high tide they appear as small off-shore islands.

*Huntsman Marine Laboratory Museum and Aquarium* in St. Andrews features live seals and exhibits of local freshwater and marine fish and invertebrates.

*Irving Nature Park* in Saint John permits the visitor to observe many species of birds and wildlife, including starfish and sea urchins inhabiting the tidal pools.

At *Magnetic Hill,* in the Magic Mountain Complex in Moncton, an

**Campobello Island**

optical illusion makes cars appear to coast uphill with the motor turned off. Magic Mountain Water Park has a wave pool, speed and twister slides and miniature golf courses.

*Miramichi Atlantic Salmon Museum* in Doaktown interprets the past, present and future relationship between people and the Atlantic salmon.

*Popes Museum,* in Grande-Anse, is the only museum in North America devoted to papal history. It includes pictures of the 264 popes and a miniature replica of St. Peter's Square and Basilica in Rome.

*Sackville Waterfowl Park* in Sackville is situated on a major migratory bird flyway. Its boardwalks allow visitors to view the varied waterfowl and other wildlife attracted by the flooded Tantramar marsh habitat.

# Significant Dates

**1534** Jacques Cartier explores the coast of New Brunswick, sailing into and naming the Bay of Chaleur.

**1604** The French attempt their first settlement in North America, on St. Croix Island.

**1635** Charles de la Tour is granted large tract of land which includes Saint John Harbour.

**1654** Nicolas Denys receives commission as Governor of Acadia.

**1713** Treaty of Utrecht awards Acadia to Britain.

**1751** Fort Beauséjour is built by the French to challenge British claims on Acadia.

**1755** Fort Beauséjour is captured and renamed Fort Cumberland.

**1755** The order for the deportation of the Acadians is proclaimed.

**1760** The Battle of Restigouche, the last battle between France and Britain for possession of Canada, is waged.

**1764** Exiled Acadians are permitted to return to Nova Scotia.

**1765** Colonial government grants over half a million acres (200 000 ha) of Maliseet lands to settlers.

**1783** 7000 Loyalists land at Parr Town (Saint John).

**1784** The Province of New Brunswick is established.

**1785** Saint John becomes the first incorporated city in Canada.

**1786** The first legislature opens in Saint John.

**1800** Kings College (now University of New Brunswick) is founded.

**1812** Napoleonic Wars give tremendous boost to New Brunswick's timber industry.

**1815** 500 former slaves from the United States arrive at Saint John and settle in Loch Lomond.

**1820** The Bank of New Brunswick, the first chartered bank in Canada, is established.

**1825** The Great Miramichi Fire, which rages for nearly three weeks, leaves over 15 000 people homeless.

**1826** Saint John creates the first paid police force in Canada.

**1842** Boundary between Maine and New Brunswick settled by the Webster-Ashburton Treaty.

**1854** New Brunswick gets responsible government.

**1864** Collège Saint-Joseph opens in Memramcook.

**1867** New Brunswick enters Confederation.

**1867** First issue of *Le Moniteur Acadien*, first French-language newspaper in the Maritimes, is published.

**1870** Canada's first YWCA is opened in Saint John.

**1875** Grace Annie Lockhart becomes the first woman in the British Empire awarded a Bachelor's degree, from Mount Allison University.

**1875** Two men die in the Caraquet Riots over the Common Schools Act.

| | |
|---|---|
| **1876** | Intercolonial Railway from New Brunswick to Montreal is completed. |
| **1877** | The Great Fire in Saint John leaves 15 000 people homeless. |
| **1881** | First Acadian Congress is held in Memramcook. |
| **1884** | Acadian national flag is adopted. |
| **1888** | Enterprise Foundry starts manufacturing stoves in Sackville. |
| **1910** | Chocolate bar invented by Ganong brothers in St. Stephen. |
| **1912** | Édouard LeBlanc becomes first Acadian appointed Bishop in New Brunswick. |
| **1918** | New Brunswick creates first Department of Health in Canada. |
| **1919** | New Brunswick women win the right to vote in provinial elections. |
| **1927** | The Maritimes Freight Rates Act reduces rail freight rates for the Maritime provinces. |
| **1929** | CFBO Radio in New Brunswick hosts fiddler Don Messer's first broadcast |
| **1930** | Hopewell native R. B. Bennett becomes prime minister of Canada. |
| **1932** | The Royal Canadian Mounted Police assume the policing of New Brunswick. |
| **1935** | Charles G. D. Roberts becomes the first Canadian poet to be knighted. |
| **1938** | New Brunswick Labour Bill guarantees workers' right to form and join unions. |

| | |
|---|---|
| **1944** | New Brunswick's North Shore Regiment lands at St-Aubain, France, as part of the D-Day invasion. |
| **1952** | A major lead-zinc depost is discovered near Bathurst. |
| **1960** | Louis Robichaud is the first Acadian elected premier of New Brunswick. |
| **1963** | The Université de Moncton is founded. |
| **1965** | New Brunswick's provincial flag is adopted. |
| **1969** | Official Languages Act makes New Brunswick Canada's only bilingual province. |
| **1970** | Richard Hatfield is elected Premier. |
| **1971** | Hédard Joseph Robichaud becomes the first Acadian Lieutenant-Governor. |
| **1973** | Ron Turcotte of Grand Falls wins horseracing's Triple Crown riding the legendary Secretariat. |
| **1979** | Antonine Maillet, Acadian author of *La Sagouine* and *Pélagie-la-Charrette*, wins the French Prix Goncourt. |
| **1987** | The Liberal Party wins all 58 seats in the New Brunswick Legislature. |
| **1992** | New Brunswick's status as a bilingual province is enshrined in the Canadian Constitution. |
| **1993** | Agreement to build a bridge between New Brunswick and PEI is signed. |
| **1994** | Congrès Mondial Acadien (Acadian World Congress) is held in southeast New Brunswick. |

**Max Aitken**

**Joseph Augustine**

**Richard B. Bennett**

**Edith Butler**

# Important People

**Max Aitken** (Lord Beaverbrook) (1879-1964), born in Newcastle; author, financier, publisher; following considerable business success in the Maritimes, moved to England where he was elected to Parliament in 1910; held cabinet posts during both world wars; awarded peerage, 1917; benefactions include the Beaverbrook Art Gallery and Playhouse Theatre. Winston Churchill considered him a "man of exceptional genius"

**Joseph M. Augustine** (1911- ), born at Big Cove; Native leader and historian; Chief (1952-54 and 1956-58) and Band Councillor (1960-64 and 1966-72) at Red Bank Reserve; discovered the Augustine Mound, a trove of artifacts dating back more than 2400 years; in 1988, received the provincial Minister's Award for Heritage

**Richard Bedford Bennett** (1870-1947), born in Hopewell; lawyer, politician; moved west in 1897; represented Calgary in the Assembly of North-West Territories and the Alberta Legislature, and was elected to Parliament in 1911. Prime minister of Canada from 1930 to 1935; moved to England in 1939

**Andrew Blair** (1844-1907), born in Fredericton; politician; premier of New Brunswick 1883-96; built provincial Liberal Party and enforced party discipline; resigned as premier to accept federal portfolio of railways and canals in the Laurier administration

**Bruno Bobak** (1923- ), Polish-born artist, immigrated to Canada in 1925; director of Art Centre of University of New Brunswick, Fredericton, 1962; awarded Silver Jubilee Medal, 1978; expands upon expressionist style in powerful oils, drawings and woodcuts.

**Molly Lamb Bobak** (1922- ), Vancouver-born artist; only woman appointed war artist in Second World War; began teaching at University of New Brunswick, 1960; employs rich imagery in art, writing, and radio and television work.

**Miller Brittain** (1912-1968), born in Saint John; artist; interest focussed on subjects of social or religious interest, using both realist and surrealist styles; earned label "the Canadian Breughel" for his sympathetic depiction of working-class life

**Edith Butler** (1942- ), born in Paquetville; recording artist; since 1973 has composed in a blended folk and rock style; co-founder of Editions d'Acadie publishers; has toured internationally

**Dalton Camp** (1920- ), born in Woodstock; political activist, author, journalist; as national president of Conservative Party, 1964-68, spearheaded leadership review leading to resignation of leader John Diefenbaker in 1966; author of *Gentlemen, Players and Politicians* (1970), about New

Brunswick politics in the 1950s and 1960s

**Bliss Carman** (1861-1929), born in Fredericton; poet; possessed a gift for startling, lyrical poetry about the relationship between people and nature; considered Canada's finest poet in his lifetime

**Herménégilde Chiasson** (1946-), born in Saint-Simon; Acadian poet, playwright, filmmaker, artist; studied under sculptor Claude Roussel at Université de Moncton; received Bachelor of Fine Arts at Mount Allison University. He has attempted to counteract the folkloric image of Acadians in his work

**Alex Colville** (1920- ), born in Toronto, Ontario; painter; taught art at Mount Allison University 1946-63; his painstaking "magic realist" style employs careful measurements, precise details and cool colours; Companion of the Order of Canada

**Joseph Cunard** (1799-1865), born in Halifax, Nova Scotia; businessman, politician; brother of Samuel Cunard, founder of the steamship company; established lumbering, milling and shipbuilding firm in Chatham in the 1820s; by 1832, was one of wealthiest men in New Brunswick; sat on Legislative and Executive councils.

**Sir Howard Douglas** (1776-1861), born in England; Lieutenant-Governor in Chief, 1823-1831; encouraged

agriculture, steam navigation, lighthouse construction; in 1828, founded King's College, now the University of New Brunswick

**Gilbert Finn** (1920- ), born in Inkerman Ferry; businessman; president and later chairman of the board of Assumption Mutual Life Assurance Company (1969-87); has served on numerous boards and commissions, and as Lieutenant-Governor (1987-94)

**Robert Foulis** (1796-1866), born in Glasgow, Scotland; civil engineer, inventor, artist; invented steam fog-horn, which hoots automatically in foggy weather; in 1825, established New Brunswick's first iron foundry in Saint John; founded a School of Arts in 1838

**Julia Catherine (Beckwith) Hart** (1797-1867), born in Fredericton; novelist; wrote the popular romance *St. Ursula's Convent* when she was only 16. Released in 1824, this was the first work of fiction by a Canadian-born author to be published in Canada

**Richard Hatfield** (1931-1992), born in Woodstock; politician; premier of New Brunswick (1970-1987); won re-election three times; introduced legislation guaranteeing equality of French and English linguistic communities; personal and political scandals brought his party to a crushing defeat in 1987

**Sir John Douglas Hazen** (1860-1937), born in Oromocto; lawyer, judge, politician; member of

**Bliss Carman**

**Herménégilde Chiasson**

**Alex Colville**

**Richard Hatfield**

**K. C. Irving**

**Valentin Landry**

**Roméo LeBlanc**

**Frank McKenna**

Canadian House of Commons for Saint John (1891-96); premier of New Brunswick (1908-11); member of federal cabinet (1911-17); Chief Justice of New Brunswick (1917-35); stood up for the rights of Maritime Canada in Ottawa

**Kenneth Colin Irving** (1923-1992), born in Bouctouche; businessman; served as pilot in World War I; rose quickly from car salesman to owner of a service station chain that launched a business empire of over 300 companies. Irving holdings range from gasoline, pulp and paper, trucking and forestry, to radio stations and newspapers, with an estimated total worth of $6 billion

**George King** (1839-1901), born in Saint John; lawyer, judge; represented Saint John in House of Assembly from 1867 to 1878; introduced Free Schools Act in 1871; appointed judge of Supreme Court of New Brunswick in 1880; appointed to Supreme Court of Canada in 1893

**Sir Pierre-Amand Landry** (1846-1916), born in Memramcook; lawyer, politician, judge; first Acadian Cabinet Minister and first knighted Acadian; MLA from 1870 to 1874 and again in early 1880s; as MP for Kent County, lobbied for Acadians and New Brunswick; appointed New Brunswick Supreme Court judge in 1893

**Valentin Landry** (1844-1919),

born in Pokemouche; teacher, school inspector, journalist; as first Acadian school inspector (1879-87), encouraged growth of Acadian schools; founded regional Acadian weekly newspaper, *L'Évangeline,* in 1887

**Arthur LeBlanc** (1906-1985), born in Dieppe; violinist, composer; recognized as a prodigy at age five; known as the "Acadian poet of the violin" for his purity of tone and expressiveness

**Msgr. Édouard Leblanc** (1870-1935), born in St. Bernard, Digby County, Nova Scotia; first Acadian bishop; appointed by Rome to Saint John diocese in 1912, following a 40-year battle by leaders of the Acadian community

**Roméo LeBlanc** (1927-), born in Memramcook; politician; Member of Parliament (1974-84); Minister of Fisheries (1974-82); summoned to the Senate in 1984, named speaker in 1993; first Acadian Governor General, appointed in 1994

**Harrison McCain** (1927- ), born in Florenceville; businessman; CEO and Chairman of the Board of McCain Foods Limited; started frozen food business in Florenceville in 1956 with brother Wallace; on boards of directors of Bank of Nova Scotia and Beaverbrook Art Gallery; Officer of the Order of Canada, 1984

**Margaret Norrie McCain** (1934- ), born in Noranda, Quebec; philanthropist; wife of Wallace McCain; appointed first woman Lieutenant-Governor of New Brunswick, 1994; founding member of the Muriel McQueen Fergusson Foundation for the elimination of family violence; member of the board of directors of several organizations, including the National Ballet School and the National Capital Commission

**Wallace McCain** (1930- ), born in Florenceville; businessman; former co-CEO and President of McCain Foods Limited; started frozen food business in Florenceville in 1956 with brother Harrison; on boards of directors of Royal Bank of Canada and Alliance for Drug-Free Canada; inducted into Canadian Business Hall of Fame, 1993

**Frank McKenna** (1948- ), born in Apohaqui; lawyer, politician; won election to the provincial legislature in 1982; became leader of Liberal party of New Brunswick in 1985. Won a clean sweep of the Legislative Assembly in 1987

**Antonine Maillet** (1929- ), born in Bouctouche; author; Companion of the Order of Canada; received Governor General's Award (1972) for *Don l'Orignal*; first writer outside France to receive the Prix Goncourt (for *Pélagie-la-Charrette*). The narrator of her works often represents the collective memory of the Acadian people

**Anna Malenfant** (1905-1988), born in Shediac; contralto,

teacher, composer; studied in Boston, Paris and Naples; started the *Trio lyrique* in Montreal in 1932; recognized for a voice of unusual beauty and naturalness; under the name "Marie Lebrun," composed *Huits chants acadiens* inspired by the region of her birth

**Don Messer** (1909-1973), born in Tweedside; fiddler; began playing at age 5; played his first radio show in 1929. In 1959 "Don Messer's Jubilee" started its ten-year run on CBC television. Developed the unslurred fiddling style of English New Brunswick

**Graydon Nicholas** (1946- ), born on Tobique Reserve, Victoria County; lawyer, judge; appointed Provincial Court Judge for Woodstock, 1991; first aboriginal lawyer in Atlantic Canada; first aboriginal judge in Maritime provinces; has concentrated on aboriginal issues and treaty rights

**Alden Nowlan** (1933-1983), born in Hartland; journalist, author, poet; left school at age 15; worked as a labourer, then as a newspaper writer and editor; his poetry collection *Bread, Wine and Tears* won the Governor General's Award in 1967

**Peter Paul** (1902-1989), born in Woodstock; barrel-maker, expert in Maliseet language and culture; advisor to many linguists and anthropologists; awarded honorary doctorate by the University of New Brunswick in

**Antoine Maillet**

**Anna Malenfant**

**Don Messer**

**Alden Nowlan**

**Pascal Poirier**

**Marcel-François Richard**

**Sir Charles Roberts**

**Brenda Robertson**

1970 in recognition of his enormous contribution to Native scholarship; Member of the Order of Canada

**Pascal Poirier** (1852-1933), born in Shediac; writer, senator; first Acadian appointed to the Senate (1885); wrote books on Acadian history and language; honoured as a Chevalier de la Légion d'Honneur by France in 1902 for his contributions to survival of French language in Acadia

**Father Marcel-François Richard** (1847-1915), born in St. Louis de Kent; priest; instrumental in founding a classical college (the Académie Saint-Louis), and building churches and convents; strong advocate of formation of Acadian diocese and appointment of Acadian bishop; known as the "Father of Modern Acadia"

**David Adams Richards** (1950- ), born in Newcastle; author; formerly editor of *Urchins* magazine; won Governor's General's Awards for *Lives of Short Duration* (1981) and *Nights Below Station Street* (1988). He gives voice to the downtrodden people of the Miramichi

**Sir Charles G.D. Roberts** (1860-1943), born in Fredericton; author, poet, professor; taught English at King's College (1885-95); considered the "Father of Canadian literature." Roberts' poems mirror the landscape of the Tantramar Marshes, and he is recognized as one of the two creators of the realistic animal story

**Brenda Mary Robertson** (1929- ), born in Sussex; politician; first woman elected to New Brunswick legislature (1967); as Minister of Youth and Social Services (1970-74), was the first woman cabinet minister in New Brunswick; Minister of Health, 1975-82; appointed to Senate, 1984

**Hon. Louis J. Robichaud** (1925-), born in St. Anthony; politician; elected to the New Brunswick legislature in 1952; chosen as Liberal party leader in 1958; 1960-70, restructured provincial government, introduced the Program of Equal Opportunity, and passed the Official Languages of New Brunswick Act

**Sir Samuel Leonard Tilley** (1818-1896), born in Gagetown; politician; delegate to Charlottetown and Québec conferences; leader of pro-Confederation forces and architect of British North America Act; held federal cabinet portfolios and twice served as Lieutenant-Governor

**Peter Veniot** (1863-1936), born in Richibucto; lawyer, politician; represented Gloucester in the Legislative Assembly (1894-1900); the first Acadian to act as premier (1923-25); Postmaster General of Canada (1926-30)

**John Clarence Webster** (1863-1950), born in Shediac; surgeon, historian; wrote medical and scientific treatises; upon retirement from medicine, turned to historical research and helped found museums at Saint John and Fort Beauséjour

**Lemuel Allan Wilmot** (1809-1878), born in Sunbury County; statesman, jurist; Attorney General (1847-1851); virtual head of first New Brunswick administration under responsible government, a reform he had advocated; judge of Supreme Court of New Brunswick; Lieutenant-Governor (1868-73)

**Sir Leonard Tilley**

## New Brunswick Premiers Since Confederation

| | | |
|---|---|---|
| Andrew R. Wetmore | Confederation Party | 1867-1870 |
| George King | Conservative | 1870-1871 |
| George L. Hatheway | Conservative | 1871-1872 |
| George King | Conservative | 1872-1878 |
| John James Fraser | Conservative | 1878-1882 |
| Daniel Hanington | Conservative | 1882-1883 |
| Andrew Blair | Liberal | 1883-1896 |
| James Mitchell | Liberal | 1896-1897 |
| Henry Emmerson | Liberal | 1897-1900 |
| Lemuel Tweedie | Liberal | 1900-1907 |
| William Pugsley | Liberal | March-April 1907 |
| Clifford Robinson | Liberal | 1907-1908 |
| John Douglas Hazen | Conservative | 1908-1911 |
| James K. Flemming | Conservative | 1911-1914 |
| George J. Clarke | Conservative | 1914-1917 |
| James A. Murray | Conservative | February-April 1917 |
| Walter Foster | Liberal | 1917-1923 |
| Peter J. Véniot | Liberal | 1923-1925 |
| John Baxter | Conservative | 1925-1931 |
| Charles D. Richards | Conservative | 1931-1933 |
| Leonard Percy Tilley | Conservative | 1933-1935 |
| Allison Dysart | Liberal | 1935-1940 |
| John B. McNair | Liberal | 1940-1952 |
| Hugh John Flemming | Conservative | 1952-1960 |
| Louis J. Robichaud | Liberal | 1960-1970 |
| Richard B. Hatfield | Conservative | 1970-1987 |
| Frank J. McKenna | Liberal | 1987- |

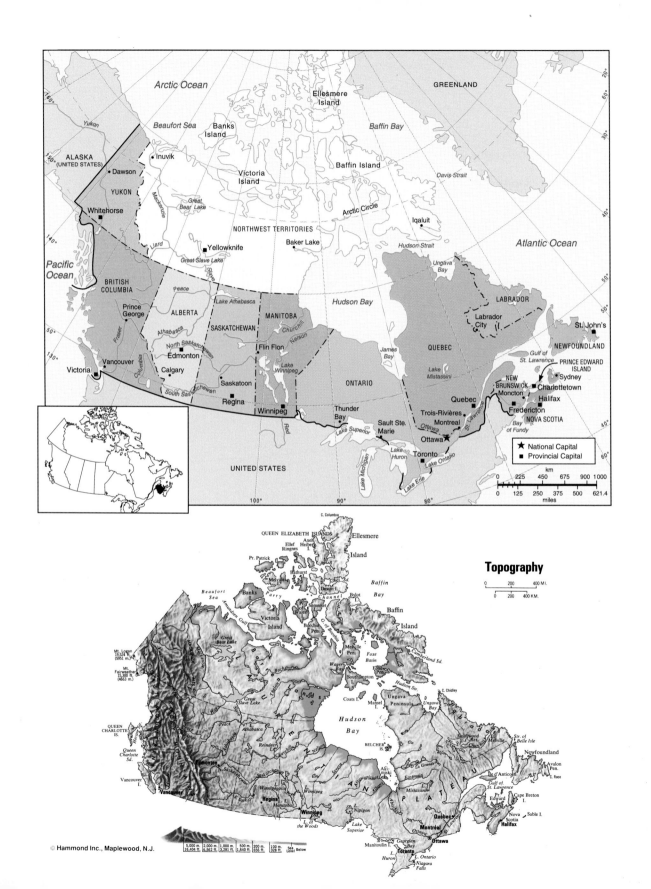

**Topography**

© Hammond Inc., Maplewood, N.J.

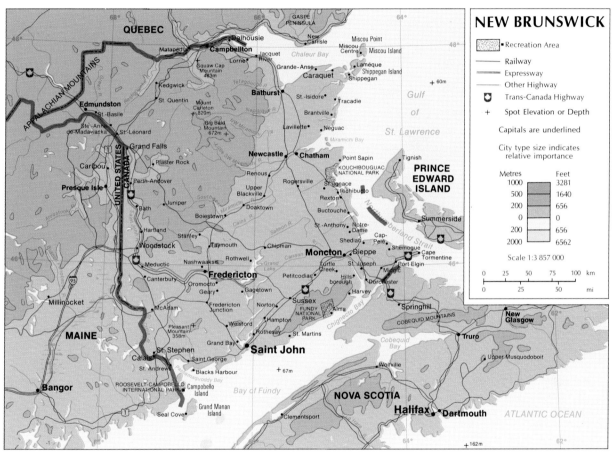

# NEW BRUNSWICK

- Recreation Area
- —— Railway
- ═══ Expressway
- —— Other Highway
- Trans-Canada Highway
- + Spot Elevation or Depth

Capitals are underlined

City type size indicates relative importance

| Metres | Feet |
|--------|------|
| 1000 | 3281 |
| 500 | 1640 |
| 200 | 656 |
| 0 | 0 |
| 200 | 656 |
| 2000 | 6562 |

Scale 1:3 857 000

0 25 50 75 100 km

0 25 50 mi

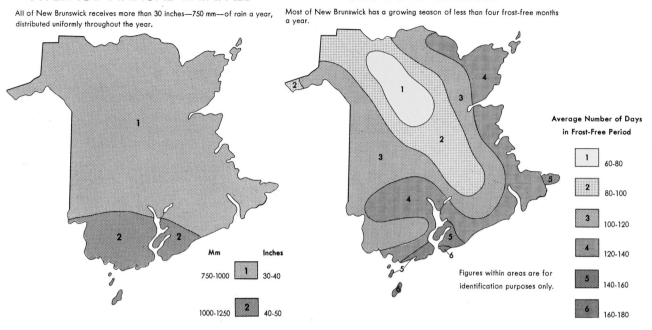

## AVERAGE ANNUAL RAINFALL

All of New Brunswick receives more than 30 inches—750 mm—of rain a year, distributed uniformly throughout the year.

| Mm | | Inches |
|---|---|---|
| 750-1000 | 1 | 30-40 |
| 1000-1250 | 2 | 40-50 |

Figures within areas are for identification purposes only.

## GROWING SEASON

Most of New Brunswick has a growing season of less than four frost-free months a year.

**Average Number of Days in Frost-Free Period**

| 1 | 60-80 |
|---|---|
| 2 | 80-100 |
| 3 | 100-120 |
| 4 | 120-140 |
| 5 | 140-160 |
| 6 | 160-180 |

Figures within areas are for identification purposes only.

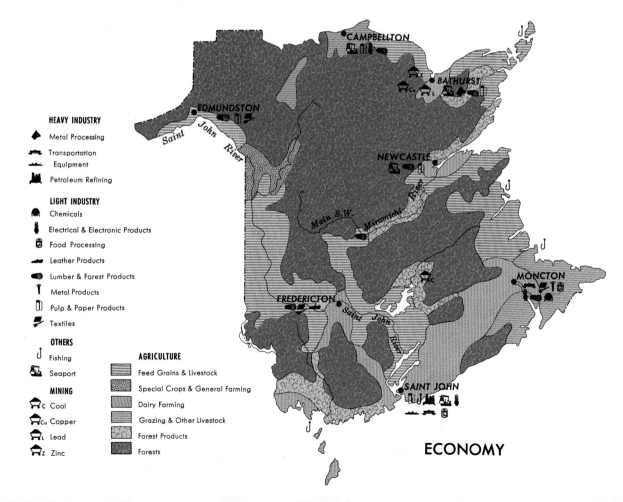

**HEAVY INDUSTRY**
- Metal Processing
- Transportation Equipment
- Petroleum Refining

**LIGHT INDUSTRY**
- Chemicals
- Electrical & Electronic Products
- Food Processing
- Leather Products
- Lumber & Forest Products
- Metal Products
- Pulp & Paper Products
- Textiles

**OTHERS**
- Fishing
- Seaport

**MINING**
- c Coal
- Cu Copper
- L Lead
- Z Zinc

**AGRICULTURE**
- Feed Grains & Livestock
- Special Crops & General Farming
- Dairy Farming
- Grazing & Other Livestock
- Forest Products
- Forests

CAMPBELLTON
BATHURST
EDMUNDSTON
NEWCASTLE
MONCTON
FREDERICTON
SAINT JOHN

Saint John River
Main S.W. Miramichi River
Saint John River

## ECONOMY

# Index

## About the Author

Marjorie Gann is a writer and teacher who lives in Sackville, New Brunswick. She began her teaching career at the Toronto French School in 1970. Since 1976, she has taught grades four through six just over the New Brunswick border in Amherst, Nova Scotia. She has developed many reading and writing programmes for elementary children, and has written articles about language arts education. She has a special interest in children's literature, and reviews children's books regularly for the journal *Canadian Children's Literature*.

### Picture Acknowledgments

Abbreviations for location on page are, alone or in combination: T = Top, M = Middle, B = Bottom, L = Left, R = Right, I = Inset, BG = Background.

Front cover, 6, 8, 12TR, 15BR, 62, 66L, 68, 73TL/BL, 75R, 79BR, 85, 86R, 93L, 94TR/BR/ML/BL, 96TR/L, 98 (all). 101 (both), 105R, 111, back cover, Malak/**Ivy Images;** 2-3, 10BR, 17, Derek Trask, **The Stock Market Inc., Toronto;** 4, 12L, 64R, 70L, 75L, 96TL, George Hunter/**Ivy Images;** 5, 16R, 58B, 70R, 71 (both), 73R, 77, 79L/TR, 81L, 93M, 99R, 100TR, 103TL/BL, 105TL/BL, 113, **Barrett & MacKay;** 10TR, 14, 100BR, Ron Garnett/**Birds Eye View;** 10L, 81R, 104TL, John Sylvester/**First Light;** 11L, 12BR, 100BL, T. Freda/**Visual Contact;** 11R, 66R, Winston Fraser/**Ivy Images;** 15TL/BL, 106 (bird/flower), 109, **Bill Ivy;** 15TR, 51L, 93R, 96B, 104BL, 105I, **Tourism New Brunswick;** 16L, 60, 61L, 84TL, 116MT, **Cathy Carnahan;** 18, **National Gallery of Canada, Ottawa;** 20, 23, 28, **Gerald Lazare and Lewis Parker;** 25 (C11237), 29 (C24550), 30 (C19584), 32 (C3552), 36 (C810), 37B (C17), 38 (C11239), 40T (C41071), 40B (C17505), 42B (C35482), 57 (PA114482), 116T (PA6467), 116MB (C7733), 117T (C25816), 120MB (C25611), 121T (PA25549), **National Archives of Canada;** 26, **Nova Scotia Museum;** 34, **The Confederation Life Gallery of Canadian History;** 37T, 42T, 46, **New Brunswick Museum;** 44 (all), 86L, 89R, 100TL, Giles Daigle/**Ivy Images;** 47 (P78/93), 55T (P37/506), 55B (P338/1), 92L (P338/5), 92R (P71/27), **Provincial Archives of New Brunswick;** 49, Carl Steeves/**Tourism New Brunswick;** 51R, 104R, Andre Gallant/**Tourism New Brunswick;** 52, 64L, Nik Wheeler/**First Light;** 58T, Walter Parker/**Hot Shots;** 61R, *Saint John Telegraph;* 75I, R. Vroom/**Ivy Images;** 82, G. Georgokakos/**Beaverbrook Gallery;** 84R, **Beaverbrook Gallery;** 84BL, **Dale McBride;** 87R, **Theatre New Brunswick;** 87L, **Théâtre populaire d'Acadie;** 89L, **Michel Tremblay;** 90, Guy DuBois/**Théâtre du rideau vert;** 94TR, 99L, 102L, 112, Brian Atkinson/**Tourism New Brunswick;** 94MR, **Peter Walsh;** 102M, **Ivy Images;** 102R, **Miramichi Folk Festival;** 103TR, Ken Straiton/**First Light;** 103BR, Peter d'Angelo/**Ivy Images;** 106BG, George K. Peck/**Ivy Images;** 116B, 117MT, 118MT/MB, 119MT, 120T/MT, **Université de Moncton;** 117MB, Diane McConnell/**Art Gallery of Ontario;** 117B, 118B, **New Brunswick Premier's Office;** 118T, **courtesy of Irving Oil;** 119T, Guy DuBois/**courtesy of Antoine Maillet;** 119MB, CBC; 119B, Kathleen Flanagan/**University of New Brunswick;** 120B, **courtesy of Senator Brenda Robertson.**